A Spirit
In the Doorway

Early Reviews from Readers of…

A Spirit in the Doorway—

"A Spirit in the Doorway" provides us with real, heart-touching demonstrations of a love shared beyond the veil of death. The love, laughter, and comfort that Childs continues to experience with her deceased soul mate give us all hope that the circle of love never ends."

—**Linda Drake,** Spiritual Medium and Life Path Healer; Author of "The Secret Pathway to Healing" and "Reaching Through the Veil to Heal"

"After recently losing someone very close to me, I was inspired by reading the stories in *A Spirit in the Doorway* to look for signs from my loved one and was surprised to recognize some! I recommend that anyone who has suffered a loss read this book to help lift their grief with new, hopeful expectations."

—**Deborah J. Johnston,** President, Care Advantage and Author of
The School of Heart Knocks

"*A Spirit in the Doorway* is a beautiful, heartfelt memoir that shows the many ways Spirit can communicate with us and illustrates how we know that our loved ones are always with us. I had many 'Aha moments' while reading this book, as the stories resonated so much with my own experiences. Thank you, Deb, for sharing the truth that so many of us recognize."

—**Lynda Matthews,** Author of *A Breath Away – A Journey Through
Love, Loss, and the Afterlife.*

"Is it possible to connect with a loved one after they cross over? Deb Childs proves to us, again and again, through her experiences with her soul mate, William, in the years since his death that if you believe it and remain open to it, you can and will!"

—**Julie Hazlett,** Realtor and Home Sales Consultant

A Spirit
In the Doorway

Amazing Ways Our Loved Ones Use Afterlife Messages To

Help Heal Our Grief

A Memoir

_____

Deborah W. Childs

A SPIRIT IN THE DOORWAY:
Amazing Ways Our Loved Ones Use Afterlife Messages To Help Heal Our Grief
Copyright © 2015 by Deborah W. Childs
A follow up to Last Promise: Losing My Heart ~ Finding My Soul
Copyright © 2015 by Deborah W. Childs

Cover Design by David Landis
Graphics Design: Landis Productions, LLC
www.landisproductions.com

Disclaimer: The following stories are told from the author's perspective and are based solely on her observations and memories. Every detail is factual and intended only to demonstrate that love and life continue after the physical life of the body ends. The stories are obviously not a promise to heal grief. One should visit a licensed professional to assist with the healing process if necessary.

ISBN 978-0-9965791-1-7
Spiritual Ink Publishing
www.debwchilds.com

"William's Dream Lives On"
A portion of all books sold will go towards an academic scholarship set up at **J. Sargeant Reynolds Community College** in Richmond, Virginia to help students who want to further their education in pursuit of a vocational trade.
JSR Donation Link can be found at
www.debwchilds.com

Dedicated To
Cameron and Grayson—
The Sons that Shine My Life

William A. Sutton, Sr.

An extraordinary child of God and the love of my life, for all that he taught me about love, life, and the continuation of love after the physical life ends.

"And think not you can direct
the course of love,
for love, if it finds you worthy,
directs your course."
~ Kahlil Gibran ~

"William's Dream Lives On"
The William A. Sutton, Sr. Memorial Scholarship Fund
www.debwchilds.com

Special Acknowledgments

Many thanks for the generosity of the esteemed authors of **"Hello From Heaven!"** —**Bill Guggenheim and Judy Guggenheim**—for their warm wishes and permission to quote from their self-published book, The ADC Project, copyright 1995, P.O. Box 916070, Longwood, Florida 32791-6070.

Bill and Judy are leaders in the field of after-death communication research, and their work is both enlightening and a blessing to those of us in grief and needing answers for healing. I turned to their work often as a resource in my time of pain, and I highly recommend their respected work and insight. Connect with them on **Facebook@ Hello From Heaven—After-Death Communication**.

Warmest appreciation to Medium, **Linda Drake**, for reading my book; the stories in it may never have come to fruition, if not for her. Had she not shown up 'right on time' to reopen the communication between William and me so beautifully after his transition, I may not have been able to grasp the degree to which he could connect with me from the afterlife. The session with Linda was a turning point in my grief recovery. I hold her in deep respect and gratitude and highly recommend her services. www.LindaDrakeConsulting.com
Linda is the author of "**The Secret Pathway to Healing**" and "**Reaching Through the Veil to Heal**"

Contents

Contents

~*~

"Because we had been together so many times before, it was easy; we just fit together. And, we knew right from the beginning that we fit together."

"You'll heal and you'll love, but it's not over between us...we'll be back together again."

—William
Through Medium, Linda Drake
October 22, 2007

~*~

Introduction
Why I Changed My Mind about Talking to the "Dead"

They say it is rare for twin-flame souls to incarnate at the same time. Most often, they have supported each other through previous lifetimes and afterwards from separate dimensions. But when they do meet again in the same space and time, it is because they have a special purpose to actuate together (More on that in my first book—Last Promise). I feel certain that William and I were twin souls. I was told by a very accurate and intuitive astrologist that we had lived many lifetimes together. She said he was in my life this time to protect me. I believe he did, and still does. I felt his desire to take care of me from the very beginning of our relationship.

But, as a twice-divorced, single mother of two young sons, I was determined to raise them as a successful and self-sufficient entrepreneur. I wanted to be the one instilling character values and sharing important childhood events with my children, rather than a hired caregiver. Many times, finances were tight, and William would plead with me, "Why won't you let me help you?" But, I needed to prove that I could take care of myself and my family after the second divorce. However, knowing that William 'had my back' enabled me to grow the confidence I needed in myself and my abilities and helped me soar to heights previously unimagined, career-wise.

With his encouragement, I stepped out and bought a business magazine, though I had never written a word for public consumption or developed any ties to the business community in my hometown. He believed in me so strongly that I believed in me, and I became very successful and financially stable due to the gamble I had taken. William was loyal, honest, very hard-working, and disciplined, and he longed for us to be married. I knew there was nobody more compatible or better for me than William, and I loved him with all my heart, yet I put marriage off for another day....a day that would never come.

William loved to help other people and felt he was doing so by being an exceptionally professional painter of homes after he retired early from a management position at a local printing company where he was the very first black supervisor. His work as an entrepreneur and painter was indeed exceptional and gave him much joy, as he used his artistic abilities and extraordinary good taste in picking paint colors to beautify homes. He gained quite a following as his customers raved about him and his work, so there was never a job shortage for him. I included an article about him and his company in my very first issue of my new magazine, which highlighted companies of excellence. The title of his article was "A Stroke of Magic," and that, William was! Charisma is an understatement when used to describe his magnetism, charm, and energy levels. I often referred to William as the energizer bunny for the huge amount of work he could accomplish in such a short amount of time.

Twin-flame souls, as explained by Plato in ancient Greece, are the result of a soul that was split into two upon creation—each a perfect reflection of the other. They spent lifetimes searching for each other to complete their whole. Plato said, **"When one of them meets his other half, the actual half of himself, the pair are lost in an amazement of love and friendship and intimacy."** And so it was with us.

We had so many things in common that the concept of twin souls makes a lot of sense to me. I only learned of the term after William was gone. We were both Libras, born a month apart in the fall. People commented on what a good-looking couple we were, due in part to, Venus, the Goddess of beauty and ruler of our sign. We both approached life logically and fair-mindedly and appreciated those values in others. We shared a great love of laughter and humor between us, which was such a blessing in our relationship. We could joke in an irreverent way about each other that never offended, and we laughed at ourselves and each other often. If we went long without laughing, William would call us out, saying, "We haven't laughed lately."

Life with William was such boisterous fun and always an adventure, and our short time together was filled with romance and many firsts—of travel to distant places, special rock concerts, symphonies, political events, and lots of beautiful, ordinary times spent at home together. Though we never got to get married, our time together was the happiest of my life. I know we were very good for each other; and losing my twin soul—again—was undoubtedly the hardest and saddest time of my life.

The story of our journey together from the strange beginning to our crisis-filled end can be found in my first book, recently retitled, **"Last Promise: "Losing My Heart ~ Finding My Soul."** Besides being a mysterious and endearing love story, it will give you a better picture of how William's personality remained intact after death. You will also receive life-affirming information you very well may not know. Bringing that awareness into the light is the "purpose part" of our reunion in this lifetime.

The story won an international writing award immediately after it was released to the world in 2011 (with a nudge from William) and has been featured in an international publication and distributed through parts of Europe since then. Readers have described it as "easy-to-read" and "hard to put down." As you will see, William was and still is electric!!

Before losing William, I never felt the need or the desire to have contact with anyone who had left the planet. Perhaps a few, too scary movies and books in my time had left indelible impressions of the 'spooky' spirit world in my psyche. To blur the boundaries between worlds seemed more than I was prepared to deal with.

That all changed when the physical absence of William tore a gaping hole in my heart and my life. He died, leaving me with enormous grief and a pressing need to communicate with him. And so, that is when my journey into a study of the afterlife began. I thought when I could no longer see him with my eyes that I would only have the memories of his great love to keep him close to me. But once he was no longer visible in my world, I soon found out that I was wrong; just because I could not *see* him did not mean that I could not *communicate* with him, and he with me. Oh! What joy came with that realization!

The astounding messages, signs, and events described in this book surprised and thrilled me and are accurate and true in every detail. I think what surprised me the most was how rapidly William could respond to me, which only proved without a doubt, that he could hear my very thoughts. He seemed to be with me constantly in the beginning, and never too far away as time went on. I learned to live again, moment-by-moment, as his messages slowly awakened me from my grieving slumber. I felt as though William was having as much fun as he did in life, intentionally surprising me with gifts that kept me smiling and moving forward, one step and message at a time.

I began to see that he was always as close as my mind, and when I thought of him, I knew he could hear me and was thinking of me, too. That blessing was greater than words can express to the grieving, sad soul that I had become. William put me on a joyful, spiritual journey and changed how I view the world today.

My wish is that anyone who reads about my experiences and has suffered great loss will be opened to the reality that love and life continue beyond this world! I am not a practicing psychic, nor do I have any special abilities that set me apart from any other person. Let this knowledge heal your heart and move your life forward to more beautiful tomorrows than previously imagined.

In the Beginning

"Don't cry because it's over. Smile because it happened"

~Ted Geisel, better known as Dr. Seuss

~ One ~

What Happened Next

Where is William?

"William is gone." I can still hear his brother-in-law's sad words exploding in my mind, initiating the awful, empty feeling in the pit of my stomach; September 11, 2007, 10:10 pm – my own personal time of terror. Grayson, my then 14-year-old-son, and I had just returned from the hospital where we said our good-byes to William about an hour before. When we got the news of William's death, Grayson tearfully recalled how he had heard of people hanging on to life waiting for someone to come and say good-bye before they died. We knew that was what had just happened.

Hot tears filled my eyes, but there was no expression on the face of my lost soul. I felt dead, too. The worst moment of my life, up to this point, was in progress. I was numb. I hugged Grayson as I held the phone with Cameron, my older son at college, on the other end, and we all cried together through time and space for the huge void that had just filled our hearts.

After William was gone, I continued to analyze the events, reliving what went wrong and wondering why such a strong human being of immense energy and vitality died so quickly in a country that put men on the moon decades ago. Deep down I knew I could not continue traveling backwards in time, reliving every action leading up to William's death and expect to go very far forward in my own life, but there was nothing else my soul would allow at the time. I felt like a confused television viewer lost in a Twilight Zone episode from the 1960's, waiting for Rod Sterling to explain the mysterious twist of fate at the end of a made-up tale about events that had occurred "somewhere out there in a dimension otherwise known as the imagination." I could only wish that had been the case.

Once the funeral was over and in the unbearable silence of the aftermath, I sequestered myself in my home, spending large amounts of time in bed reading. I had piles of books about channeling spirits and all sorts of stories about the afterlife. I had never wanted to speak to or see the dead before, but now I wanted to know *where* William was and *what* he was doing.

Evidently, he was already in communication with my sons. I think William was able to get through to their open hearts and minds soon after he passed over. Grayson recounted the following shortly after William's funeral, and his story illustrates **how important it is to pay attention to what thoughts appear in your mind about your loved ones.** Otherwise, you may miss beautiful messages like this one from their hearts to yours:

"As soon as I got off the bus, I noticed how beautiful the day was. The sky was very blue, and there was a nice breeze. Immediately I thought of William. I felt the day was a metaphor for his new way of being—that after all the suffering he had gone through, I had the distinct feeling that he was okay now. He had come through the pain to a better place. I think he was letting me know."

My young son's wise words are so beautiful to me, even now, that almost eight years after-the-fact they still bring tears to my eyes. What Grayson felt made absolute sense to me because William could always tell when Grayson was worried about him. He didn't like giving a heavy burden like that to a child; he thought he was too young to carry it. I am sure he would want to relieve Grayson of the worry, like he often tried to do at the end when he was at his sickest at our home.

Grayson's heart and mind were open channels, able to receive feelings and thoughts from William. My numbed mind was a jumbled state of emotional debris gone haywire. Now I recognize that this is not the way to open a channel of communication with your dearly departed. If I could have found any way possible to bring William back from heaven, I would have tried it. Our forced separation in the end had been unbearable. I believe he chose to go comatose in protest of how all control had been taken from him by those he trusted and loved most. He was a strong man with a lot of pride. But even before we were physically separated, I had not realized that we had always been deprived of having a moment of privacy to talk to each other. I needed closure now; closure I couldn't get in the last days and hours of his life when we were apart.

One day when I did make it out of my house, I went to a local store to show a friend how well William looked in the last photographs taken of us. A sign on the door stopped me in my tracks. It was just the thing I was looking for—a spirit-channeling medium was coming to town! But, what immediately grabbed my attention was the date of the event; she was making appointments to contact loved ones on a date that was etched into my memory—October 22—the date of the **very first time William and I met at my door,** more than a decade earlier!

I recognized the relevance of the synchronicity and knew it was not to be ignored. My Divine guidance antennae shot straight up, and I felt that William wanted to communicate with me as much as I wanted to talk to him. I took action immediately; I bought the medium's book and made an appointment with her.

I was nervous about going "to hear from William." What if he doesn't show up, and I am disappointed? What if he supposedly shows up, but it doesn't sound like him, or worse—what if it is **so** much like him that I feel like I am losing him again when it is over? I had no way of knowing what to expect from the spirit realm. The day finally came for my channeling experience. My emotional protection was on high alert.

Medium, Linda Drake, is very experienced in talking to spirits. It did not take me long to see that she was the real deal. After surrounding me by the White Light of the Ascended Masters for protection and asking for truth, clarity, wisdom, and healing in all areas of my life, Linda proceeded. Immediately she asked me, **"Is it a boyfriend?"** Surprised that she picked up on the fact that William and I were not married, I nodded yes. I almost felt silly to have worn a band on my relationship finger to "test" her. Her next words touched me deeply as she continued:

"Because there is a man in the doorway with his BIG heart in his arms, and he is offering this to you; He comes in with a lot of love."

That made me smile and put me at ease. I felt a new sense of welcome anticipation. Maybe I had found a way to bring William back—at least for a conversation. This was already going better than I had anticipated. The next exchange greatly increased my certainty of William's presence.

Linda asked, **"Is he emotional?"** but before I could respond, she put up her hand and corrected herself, **"Sentimental,** he says." Now I am truly excited, recognizing William's personality in her words. I smile to myself thinking, "That IS William." Obviously, passing over does not seem to have changed his earthly persona. He would equate the word, 'emotional' with being weak, whereas being sentimental is a gift from a giving heart. Linda goes on explaining, **"That's what the big heart is; It's like a sentimental thing. He has beautiful energy."**

I smiled as I told her, "I talk to him all the time."

"He hears you. He's right there. He says, 'we both need her to talk.' He's listening, and he wants you to hear what he has to say. You'll get so you hear it more and more. You may not hear a voice; it may be in your heart, or he'll give it to you in some other way."

That would turn out to be quite an understatement. I was already getting some signs, but I didn't quite know if I was imagining things or not. After all, it was the first time I actually wanted to be contacted by anyone in the spirit world. The first hint of William's presence in the very beginning of his absence was in the otherwise unexplainable movement of a leafy plant in my kitchen one night shortly after William died. I am still surprised that I noticed it through all my tears.

I was crying out loud and calling his name, when across the room I noticed the leaves of a plant moving, as though something had caused a breeze. I stopped crying and proceeded to look for any rational explanation. The heat pump wasn't running, so there was no air circulating the space. Even after the heat did come on, it did not cause a movement in the branches of the plant. I kept my eyes peeled on the plant for a good while to see if anything else caused the leaves to move. Nothing; the leaves did not move again.

The scientist in me even went over to see if I could *create* a breeze that would cause the leaves to move, but to no avail. No one else, that I could see, was in the kitchen. Why I was even *looking* at the plant during my crying binge, I do not know. But after I noticed the movement, I became interested in an explanation and stopped crying.

Could I have been upsetting my angel? Was he trying to divert my attention to other thoughts? It only crossed my mind, but that was before I had many more incredible happenings to analyze.

~ Two ~

My Heart is Open
I Can Hear You Now
September/October, 2007

I soon learned that in the beginning of my grief state, I was too disheartened to hear anything from William. At the suggestion of the channeling medium, I met with a certified Reiki Master named Freda to "open my heart." Freda had already performed a miracle for me with advice that enabled me to say good-bye to William on his deathbed after being separated from him before he died. I figured if she could *do that*, she could do anything.

I was told that because I was crying so much, my mind was filled with the sounds of my own sobbing and could hear nothing more. However, after working with Freda, mind-to-mind interaction between William and me began to occur, and I experienced communication from him frequently, and even on request!

Now I have so many precious, post-transition memories that he has created for me! The messages I received, and still receive, are dear to me because they let me know, without a doubt, that he is still with me; not just "in my memories and in my heart," like the words on sympathy cards and spoken by well-meaning people who try to make you feel better, but in *the invisible present with me*.

Visual Message in Yoga

Being clairvoyant means being able to sense a clear vision that cannot be substantiated by the five senses in that moment. I experienced this through a yoga instructor at the gym about a month or so after William passed. I made a last-minute decision to try a yoga class. At the end of the class, Debbie, the instructor took the class through a guided meditation with a visualization exercise. You cannot imagine the look of surprise behind my eyelids when she took us to a place where William and I had been before! I recognized it immediately—a park scene with clear blue skies, yellow leaves, and the bench we sat on while watching people go by.

I was transported back in time, seeing us together early in our relationship, so happy just sitting on that park bench. I could see his pretty smile and feel how much he loved being with me and our mutual joy as we soaked up the warm sun, talking and appreciating the beauty of nature all around us. It was just as if it were happening again in that very moment.

This appeared to be the part of the yoga class where we were supposed to be in peaceful repose. But the memory was so vivid and bittersweet that all I could concentrate on, as hard as I could, was fighting back tears. I was worried what the instructor would think if she were to walk around and find one of her new student's faces contorted in pain and crying with her eyes closed during an exercise designed for serenity and relaxation, aptly known as *dead man's pose.*

I was definitely not relaxed. I apologized to her after the class. She had no idea she was having a clairvoyant experience with me. We became wonderful friends after that class, and I am still an avid fan of Studio D Yoga and Debbie, the owner/instructor, as well as, the healing art of yoga. It is exercise for the body and meditation for the mind, all at one time. And, obviously, it can take you to places you may not expect to go!

Telepathy and Musical Messages

Being clairaudient means that someone receives information with their *inner or outer* hearing. I was about to experience many more of William's messages through that form of communication—telepathy (inner hearing) and music (outer hearing).

After my yoga class, I headed over to the elliptical machines. I was a little apprehensive after my last experience and was hoping that the gym's musical selections would not bring even more tears. At first the music was spirited and not centered on relationships; I noticed and was relieved. But just as suddenly, things changed. I could see William in my mind's eye, standing in front of the elliptical machine I was on. I noticed he had on his yellow shorts and a white shirt with the arms cut out that I remembered so well. He was smiling there, just watching me. And then, *it happened.*

My mind zoned in on the words of a song that had just started playing. My legs almost stopped taking strides on the elliptical machine. I listened intently and couldn't believe how directly the song spoke to my heart. It was exactly what I felt William would say to me, and some of the words and phrases in the song were things he *actually had said* to me before.

I strained to catch and remember some of the words because while I was a big fan of current pop music, surprisingly, I had never heard the song, nor did I recognize the artist. I planned to search the internet for the words when I got home. Later I found and printed the lyrics to Ryan Cabrera's song, "Shine On." There was no question in my mind that William was using the song to speak to me.

It abruptly ended in silence on the words, **"You're gonna' be alright, Love."** I stood with my jaw hanging down, not believing how crazy meaningful the words of the song were to us and to my situation without him. I felt they were spoken from William's heart to mine. I knew that if he knew anything about me now, he knew that I was feeling like there was no purpose in my life; no desire in me to go forward without him.

In the song were words William used in life to refer to me—'beautiful' and 'love.' He now stood before me in my mind's eye using a song composed of his very expressions encouraging me to not *just* go on, but telling me that it was my destiny to "*shine* on." That I would be "better than ever" and that he would be with me "til the very end."

William made sure I would get his message that day with an attention-getting telepathic vision of him that preceded the music he wanted me to hear. He used that process several more times after that day. Whenever I would see him—in exactly the same outfit—I knew to be alert. The gym was the perfect conduit for musical messages because music played constantly (except during yoga), and I was already plugged into a channel of energy he could use. It was easy, effective, and required less energy to be expended on his part. I have read that some actions—like actual appearances—require a lot of energy by our loved ones.

I should not have been surprised that William would use songs to talk to me since we both love music and its ability to connect with us on a deeply emotional level. Since, there are infinite numbers of songs expressing every emotion ever felt; it only makes sense that a spiritual being composed of the etheric energy of heaven would use the non-physical energy of music available on earth as a tool to speak to those of us separated from them.

One may choose to see musical messages as coincidence and over-thinking on my part, but I can assure the skeptic in you that if your heart is open, you will get the message that is attempting to be conveyed to you. You will know by the relevance in the personal meaning for you. No one else can speak to that. If you are noticing it, there is a reason that only you will understand. If you never listen to music or are not a fan, your loved ones will probably not be as likely to use it as a means to communicate with you.

I imagine William having access to an all-encompassing heavenly library, looking for songs with just the right words that I had not heard before, so I would have to listen intently to remember them and research later. I would not have listened the same way if I had known the song well.

When William found a Seal song I did not know, I was astounded! He knows that I adore Seal's music and have almost all of his CDs. We even attended an outdoor Seal concert together and sat a couple rows from the stage on Brown's Island in Richmond, Virginia where I live. When, again, I "saw" William standing clearly in front of me at the gym, I began to listen up, knowing I was about to receive a message, and this one was very powerful.

The Seal song began and grabbed me from the very first words; it was titled—"Rolling." I was shocked by the eerie time-frame parallels of William's health battle to the song's reference to **"You haven't seen what I saw 17-months a year when it rained."** When I heard those words, I knew the song held a message for me about his illness and how he felt about it. I may only be getting the full meaning of the message at this moment while typing these words. (Perhaps, he is helping me edit!) It is possible that the song is more about coming to terms with the illness as the purpose for his transition back to spirit than it is about wrestling with an earthly disease, as I originally thought. What did he want me to hear from this song?

Since we did not really get a chance to talk near the end of his life, it seemed quite obvious from the song that William wanted me to understand what he went through in deciding to let go of this life. He makes it clear through the words in the song that he searched for understanding as to why he got sick and what it had to do with his purpose in life. William was always pondering out loud why he was still here when all the other men in his family had died. He wanted to know God's purpose for his life.

The song accurately indicated that he tried to keep going, to keep living, and that he wanted to live. But in the song, there is a sense of conflict with his feelings—that something had presented itself in his search for understanding his illness; that he had found what he was waiting for—**"something to lead me home."**

Many have said we ultimately have the final say when it comes to that moment of living or going on over. While I was trying so hard to keep him alive here, it seems William was looking for answers to a bigger question   why was he being called home?

The song described what I saw William do—he shut his eyes to the world. The song says **"Rolling out of my bed, I still can't find the truth I am looking for. Going back instead, I shut my eyes and dream who I can be once more."** I was told by the medium during the channeling experience that William was traveling back and forth to the Other Side when his eyes were shut to get out of the pain of the body. She said that made it easy for him to adjust to the transition when it occurred. Once when he woke up in the hospital, he told me, "I've been talking to your daddy; we talked a long time." My dad had been gone for 34 years. I thought William was experiencing the withdrawal effects of the meds at the time.

Early on in the song, as in his illness, there is a reference to being seen as someone who is searching for truth that can't be found and also of being seen as **someone who has knowing *without* understanding.** But at the end of the song, and I now believe at the end of his earthly life, William had found the truth he was searching for, and he gained both 'knowing and understanding.' It is as if he had been enlightened to his purpose, the role of the disease in his life, and what he had to do **"to live again."** He chose to be led home for a new life, a new body, and his true purpose.

The words of the mysterious Seal song made me feel, again, as though William was standing right in front of me, this time trying to make me understand that what had happened was meant to happen, and that I have to move on with my purpose like he had to with his part in the Grand Plan.

Once near the end, while he was in the hospital during a rare moment of lucidity and privacy, William tried to warn me saying, "I'm not going to be here long." He was right; soon we were separated, and within a day's time he lapsed into a coma. I did not comprehend the meaning behind that final message to me, just as I didn't understand the full meaning of this one within the Seal song the first time I thought about the words.

I know now that through this special song choice by a very special artist to me, William was explaining why he made the decision to let go of the life we had together. I believe he wanted me to understand this because he could see and feel the pain I was in with our separation. He told me through the medium that we would be together again.

As you can see, it is when our minds are still and quiet like I was in meditative yoga or without thought on an exercise machine, that those in the spirit world can get through to speak to us and have us hear them—but we must be aware and open to receive the message; that is true whether it be the Holy Spirit with a Divine message to guide us or a loved one separated by unseen dimensions in space and time. Both want the best and highest good for us. But I have learned again today, that even though we may "get" a message, it may be years before we "really get it." Patience truly is a virtue.

~ Three ~
Perfectly-Timed Messages
Speaking Through Others
October, 2007

Towards the end of William's time on earth, he was either sleeping, back in the hospital, or in crisis mode. And anyway, it was too late or inappropriately bad timing to talk about some of the subjects I longed to talk to him about at that point. You are not sure whether you will have the chance to have certain conversations, but you don't want your loved one believing that you are seeing the end of their lives for them. Because if others—including doctors—see it for them, they will see it for themselves, and it will be sped up. It is a very touchy and delicate time.

Marriage had always been one of those delicate subjects for us in good times. He wanted to get married, but after my two divorces, I was partly afraid that marriage might ruin our perfect relationship. During our last conversation about the subject in October of 2006, eight months after his cancer diagnosis, he said he'd never bring the subject up again, and as far as I can remember, he never did.

He never got to know that I had written a letter (but didn't send it because of the uncertainty of his surgery) to Regis and Kelly in February, 2006 to try and win a surprise TV wedding. He would have loved that idea when he was well. But, as he became sicker and uncertain of his future, my bringing the subject of marriage up could have been taken many ways; so I didn't. I always wished I had at least told him about my idea, so he would have known he was the man I wanted to marry. But I am sure he now knows all about it.

After William was gone, I couldn't help but wonder if he had really given up on us. Even though we were at odds with the idea of marriage, I always felt it had nothing to do with our love for each other. Sometimes I felt we were never married for reasons that went beyond our understanding. Now that he was gone, it was an eerie feeling that haunted me. I felt guilty for not marrying him years before. I could not help thinking about how he wanted to get married and our last conversation about it. I even wondered if he still loved me at the end because I knew he was bitter about it. I was heartbroken that we had not made marriage a priority of discussion, or at least made the engagement a reality to proclaim our love to the world.

I wondered why we hadn't formalized the commitment. The thought that he gave up on us becoming man and wife tormented me. I would ask my son who worked with him every day in the summer if he thought William still loved me, and he would assure me that William always said he did. Nothing ever made me feel better about it. The thought of it just made me feel incredibly sad, and I thought about it quite a lot in the time right after he died.

I Do

Around that same time period, the telephone rang one evening. One of William's last customers was on the phone. I had heard William talk about Mr. Davis, as he was always talking about his favorite customers. He had painted for the Davis' while I was in Vegas at a conference in May of 2007. I was very surprised to hear from Mr. Davis because he had never called me before, but he had an understandable question; he wanted to know if someone was going to "take up William's work and finish where he had left off?" He had given William a deposit for the work, but said that William had done so many extra things for them over the years that the money they gave him was not a problem. I gave him the name of William's close friend and painting associate.

Then for no apparent reason, before hanging up, Mr. Davis said something of great interest to me. He could not have known of its significance without heavenly help. Out-of-the-blue, he said, "You know, when William was here in May, he said if things went the way he planned, he thought he would be getting married next year."

Speechless, my jaw dropped, and I still get chills thinking about it. I had no knowledge of their conversation and unbeknownst to me, this man was able to confirm that William had not given up on marrying me! I guess I was so excited that Mr. Davis even got his wife on the phone, and she corroborated William's words. If I had ever spoken to the Davis' before, I don't remember it, but even if I had talked to them, I never would have expected to talk to them again with William gone.

I am surprised they still had my phone number or remembered my name to look it up. William had the only people with the answers to my concerns give me a call that night. There was no other explanation. He was hearing my thoughts and sad concerns. He wanted me to know that he never stopped loving me and that he loves me still. Now instead of wondering if he wanted to marry me, I just hear him saying, "I do."

Happy, Belated Birthday

On my birthday in October of 2008, I asked William to give me a sign, which was on a Thursday. I thought he didn't get the message, but the following Sunday, I was talking on the phone when another call came through, and I decided to see who it was. The caller said, "You probably don't remember me," and she told me her name was Valerie, which I immediately recognized as a customer of William's. I told her that I remembered her well. We met once at a store when I was with

William. Her next question shocked me as she asked, "Is William alive?"

The question sent chills up my spine, and I hated to give her the bad news. She sounded so sad, but said she knew in her heart that he was not alive. She said she could feel it. She said she had been looking for my number for some time. She knew that William had given it to her once, and she finally found it. How interesting that she would find it around my birthday. William knew she needed answers about him, and he could connect us and also give me a gift. Valerie and I got to share memories of someone who was special to both of us. Just like in life, William is the most efficient and productive man I have ever known!

Before Valerie and I hung up, she told me how much William wanted to get married and how much he loved me. That was the best birthday present I received that year....and that was the only time I have ever heard from Valerie.

William, Playing at the Work He Loved -- Summer, 2001

~ Four ~

My Invisible Helper

Picking out Gifts
November, 2007

William had been gone two months at this point. We were never separated for more than a week, and that was only one time, that I can recall. I still didn't feel like going anywhere, but my friend, Ellen, was hosting a charitable event in her home and wanted me to come. Items such as photography and jewelry were being sold. While I was there, I suddenly got the idea to pick out earrings as Christmas gifts for William's sisters and gift them from him. It was the first Christmas without him, and the only thing that made me feel the holiday spirit at all, was doing things in his memory.

I was having trouble deciding which earrings to give to whom, and I was silently asking him to help me with the best selection for each of his five beloved sisters. William had great taste, and I was being indecisive, as usual. Christmas music was playing softly in the background, and people were talking to each other and to me. My mind was very preoccupied with picking out the gifts and looking at jewelry for myself, when out-of-the-blue, an old R&B song suddenly popped into my head that I recognized, but never think of, and I noticed it immediately because it was so out-of-place and time.

The song was "La La Means I Love You" by the Delfonics. There was absolutely no reason for this song to occupy space in my mind at this time, except as a thank you from William for having (or receiving) the idea to remember his sisters at Christmas for him. After that experience, I found that song popping into my head or I would surprise myself by singing the tune from out of nowhere.

I believe that when the song comes to my attention, it is William's way of telling me he is thinking of me and that he loves me. We often used songs to tell each other how we felt, so this is something he can count on me noticing. I believe that's why he has used music many times to speak to me with success in delivering a message.

I read somewhere that if we want our loved ones to respond to us, we need to call their name three times to get their attention. I have not found the need to do that with William. He always seems to answer me immediately or initiate contact on his own. But I do often speak a request, both inwardly and out loud, if I want to emphasize that I really need his help as soon as possible. There is definitely power in the spoken word.

One very memorable example was a thought I got when shopping for the 30th birthday of one of his favorite nieces. He loved all his nieces in a special way, but one in particular was very close to him. She went to Church with him on Sundays and confided in him in a way she could not do with other people. He felt that she was like a daughter to him. So, I wanted to get her something memorable for her special birthday from both William and me.

I was in a specialty store, and I whispered for William to help me choose something that would hold special meaning for her. It was almost at that moment that the store clerk handed me a beautiful little heart-shaped porcelain box. It was green with a pink ribbon and sparkles on it. I knew it was perfect the minute I saw it.

Then immediately, a long-forgotten item popped right into my mind. I should say *I* had forgotten all about it, but obviously, William had not. A couple years earlier, he had found a petite emerald ring with little diamonds set around it. It looked a little young for me and maybe he could see something in my face when he gave it to me because he said, "Now, if you don't want it, let me know, I'll give it to Tam."

It was hidden away in my jewelry box in my closet, and I had not seen it since I put it there. I had never worn it, but it was special to me just because he gave it to me, especially now, under the circumstances. Out of nowhere, that conversation came flooding back to me in memory, and I knew it was because he was telling me that it would be perfect in the little pink and green box. It would also make this the most meaningful gift I could possibly give William's niece from him—and after all—that is what I asked him to help me with. I can't imagine ever thinking of that little ring without his prompting.

William's niece was very moved by the gift and its special significance to her "Uncle Ossie." Even though the ring was a little difficult to part with, because it was the only ring he had ever given me, it made me so happy to give his niece the perfect 30th birthday gift, which I know was sent from heaven with lots of love.

~ Five ~

Physical Signs

Believing is Seeing
November/December, 2007

Most people tend to believe only after they see something with their eyes, hence the saying, "Seeing is believing." However, I have found that being open to believe allowed me the possibility to notice and receive more messages from William in more amazing ways; the session with medium, Linda Drake, had opened the portal of possibility for me, and I was wide open!

After a while, William started becoming more playful and creative, adding actual physical signs to his repertoire of communication methods. He would even find ways to employ others to help him deliver incredible material gifts to me. For just as William had been masterful in removing obstacles while on earth, he was equally successful in putting his new energy to use in removing the new barriers of non-physicality between us.

He wasn't one to give up on anything he wanted to accomplish. He told me from the very beginning that he "had a knack for removing obstacles." And it would soon become obvious that nothing about that personal element of his will had changed either.

I don't really know if you have to be a higher-evolved soul to accomplish what William has done for me from the Other Side. Maybe it was related to my new receptivity, or perhaps the close, twin-soul relationship we had on earth. I do know that I have lost many people, and only one other sign from anyone else ever made its way back to me, and that was only after I started opening up to that possibility by reading about the experiences of others, like you are doing right now.

I do believe that the extent to which we receive any communication has to do with our receptiveness *to* communicating. So, if like me, you spent your life saying you did not want to have any communication with dead people because it would freak you out, then you probably won't. Our loved ones do not wish to scare us.

It may not be until the separation you experience is worse than your fear of what you cannot fathom or feel comfortable with, that you are able to open up to receive messages from your loved ones. I hope that is why you are reading this book, and if so, I believe you have a very good chance of that communication happening for you.

And Then There was Light!

One night shortly after William was gone, I awoke in my bed around 3am. The harsh reality of his absence hit me immediately—an awful memory, conveniently lost momentarily to the subconscious state of sleep. At that moment I screamed out in frustration, "WILL-YAM!!!" I closed my eyes, crying, and to my surprise, I immediately detected light behind my eyelids! I threw open my eyes to see if William was there at the foot of my bed, like sometimes happens in books about afterlife communication.

What I saw was light from the floodlight on my back deck. Disappointed, my next thought was to wonder what made that stupid light come on. It was a motion detector light, but it was very temperamental in its decision to grace us with its presence. In fact, there had been times when I jumped up and down under it, flailing my arms to trigger the necessary movement to trip it on, and still be unsuccessful.

So, what made it come on tonight? I got out of bed and stood in my Jacuzzi tub under the window for a good while trying to see if some animal would move to cause the annoying light to pop on. Nothing; I saw our cat, Susie, sleeping peacefully, with nothing moving to disturb her. So, I finally gave up and got back in bed.

The very second my eyes closed, darkness fell again behind my lids as the light popped right back off. I smiled and said, "Thank you, Babe." I knew at that moment that the annoying light had been executed with perfect timing to divert my attention from the pain in my heart to a curiosity that would calm me down—like with the leafy plant in an earlier story. I may never be able to count on that light, but I can always count on William to shine for me, just as he has both before and after his transition.

Love-Stained Art

I realize that some events might seem questionable to others as to whether William had a hand in them or not. I suppose some would see this example as wishful thinking on my part. But, truly—whether a sign, message, or event is the result of an intuitive knowing, Divine guidance, or anything else that can't be proven scientifically—the true measure of its value is about the relevance its meaning has to you, as the observer of your life, and what you believe about it. And belief is a choice, of course.

So, I share out of love because of the special place these messages have in my heart. I will say that I am somewhat of a skeptic by nature, so every event I make mention of in this book made me deeply suspect William's other-worldly participation and had an effect on me and my life.

This one has relevance to William because it involved a sudden and strange, but comforting element, which appeared during an emotional upheaval in my family home—one I know would not have happened if William had been there to keep me cool. It produced an immediate calming effect on me, and it involved my younger son.

William was a wonderful parent and never one to overreact with angry words like me. He was careful with his words because as he often warned, "Once they get out, you cannot get them back." His heart-felt message during my little crisis transformed the situation and me into the better way in which he would have handled it. My attention was grabbed by a most uncommon sign, which gave me pause to suspect his involvement. Let me explain.

I was out shopping one afternoon, about 10 minutes from home, and did not notice right away that my cell phone registered a missed call. When I returned the call, the panicked voice of my son said, "Mom, you need to come home right now! The upstairs toilet is overflowing, and I can't stop it!! Water is going everywhere!! Hurry!!"

For what seemed like the thousandth time, too much toilet paper and not enough flushes had probably caused the water in the same toilet to rise, which is why my temper rose with the news. Normally I was home at this time of day, but of course, not that day. Attempting to avert disaster, my 14-year-old son tried to do what he had seen me do in the past and took the toilet tank top off to lift the arm with the ball attached to stop the water from rising. But with the Titanic-like waves of water overflowing the bowl, he panicked, pulled up too hard and broke the arm off in his hand.

Unfortunately, he did not know about the shut-off valve. So, the water flowed over the bathroom floor, while he threw towel-after-towel atop the flood waters to try and prevent them from heading out onto the carpet in the hall. Before he could get me on the phone and I could tell him what to do, the water had already seeped through the bathroom tile floor all the way through to the kitchen ceiling downstairs. A steady stream of toilet water had filled up the base of the new chandelier over the kitchen table.

By the time I got home and the drainage had stopped, the water filled a five-gallon bucket and big brown stains were forming on both the kitchen ceiling and the adjacent family room ceiling where

William had just patched water stains a year earlier due to the *last* overflowed toilet in that bathroom; the same family room that had once been dull and boring until William reinvented it for me with bright yellow walls, colorful furnishings, and white woodwork. It was our favorite room of my home where we spent many of his last days together. He always marveled over the transition of the space and how pretty the room had become.

When I saw those stains forming, I was not a calm or compassionate mother for my traumatized son. The flood highlighted the loss of my beloved "Mr. Fix It," and for that, my son took a non-stop, verbal thrashing from me. I spared no wrath in blaming him for the disaster. I was still angrily spewing blame...... when suddenly I noticed a shape had formed on the family room ceiling.

A perfectly-shaped, water-stained heart sat on the clean white ceiling, right above where the Christmas tree would go in a few days. My wrath came to an immediate halt and was replaced by a calm, peaceful demeanor. The image was so striking that I took pictures of it. My first thoughts went straight to William. I just knew in my bones that, again, he was working his magic to calm me down through a crisis.

But this time it was to divert my anger away from my son by sending me a heart of love to soften me up. I could hear him saying, "Once they pass over your lips, you can't take them back." The heart stain worked magic on my attitude! I didn't even ***want*** it to be covered over by paint, and it wasn't for a long time. I truly cannot think of anything else that would have been able to adjust my emotions and take me out of my anger faster than that heart-felt message from my new guardian angel.

I apologized to my son because I knew it was not his intent to cause such a mess. Soon after, I ordered a replacement toilet that worked much better. And there was peace in our world for Christmas, thanks I truly believe, to our angel, William, who was still 'painting' my ceilings with his stroke of magic and a lot of love.

Message in a...Fortune Cookie?

It was Saturday morning, the first week in December. I was headed into three months without my angel, and fairly depressed, as Christmas loomed in the near future like a gaunt bird waiting for prey. I was alone and lonely. I did not want anything to do with Christmas and was definitely not into the huge task of decorating for it. William always helped me with everything. He was so speedy, getting more done in an hour than I could get done all day by myself. And that is NOT an exaggeration. Plus, there were things like the 'crazy-tree' tradition we had started with colorful light roping that would never happen again without him to climb up ladders to create it.

I didn't want to deprive my two sons of their Christmas joy, but I was having a real hard time motivating myself to climb up and down two set of stairs, drag everything out of the attic by myself, put it up, and drag it back up to the attic after Christmas. I would have loved to be able to twitch my nose like Elizabeth Montgomery on the old sitcom, "Bewitched," to make the whole season go away and be done with it. It would have been a good time to be a good witch.

I finally bribed myself into going to work out at the gym and then to the hardware store for a new tree stand, and as a treat, I would allow myself to order Chinese food, like William and I used to do sometimes on the weekends. It would be the first time since he left that I had eaten Chinese. So, I did my chores, and the food was delivered.

I was sitting on a stool at the kitchen counter watching television while I ate the same dinner I always ordered; my "twin-soul treat"—Honey Crispy Twin—shrimp and chicken in a sweet, white sauce—my favorite. And then I absentmindedly opened the fortune cookie, as usual after dinner, with no thoughts behind it. I was still engrossed in television.

I glanced down to read the fortune and saw a "word lesson" on it—a format, which I had not remembered seeing before. It had an

English word with the Chinese translation for it. The word 'boyfriend' got my immediate attention, of course. What were the chances? When I turned the fortune over to get my message, it read, "It's time to get moving—your spirits will lift accordingly."

WHAT? I thought, are you KIDDING me?? Okay, the message alone—pretty significant, considering my mental state of mind that day with Christmas bearing down over my depressed, lethargic soul and lots to get done—but, the word, BOYFRIEND, as well on the same fortune!!!!! That was too much to be a coincidence.

I had no doubt that William wanted me to know that he was with me in Spirit and was offering me the joyful motivation I lacked. It was like a "Come on now; I am here with you to get you through this." He wasn't going to be able to do the heavy lifting this year, but he *was* with me! It certainly did light up my night, and it got me through decorating for Christmas without him—in the physical.

My message to William: "I still can't believe it—you can even use *fortune cookies* to create the perfect message when you need one? How amazing must your heaven be!"

~ Six ~
Valentine Presence
Heartfelt Memories

Celebrating Valentine's Day was one of the few things William and I had a difference of opinion about in the beginning of our relationship. Holidays in general annoyed William, except for Christmas, because he felt manipulated by the commercial gift-giving machine. He liked to give gifts for no reason all year long, on any old day that pleased him. To give when something was expected took the joy of the surprise out of the giving for him, and he rebelled against the control factor.

The first Valentine's Day we were together, he ignored the day and me, altogether. Of course that hurt my feelings. I remember saying, "How can you ignore the one day of the year set aside for people who love each other?" Everyone I knew who had anyone special in their lives celebrated Valentine's Day together.

Unlike some men, who insist on maintaining their position to the detriment of the relationship, William relented and never ignored the day again. That reminds me of a definition of love put forth by the Dalai Lama, **"Love is the wish to make someone happy."** He put my feelings before his, and every year after bought me jewelry, sent me flowers, and/or took me out to dinner like the princess he treated me as every other day of the year. I was a very spoiled princess.

So, the first Valentine's Day without him was going to be hard. His beautiful sisters sent me flowers to cushion the pain. One of my friends brought me candles and another left me flowers and a monetary gift for William's Scholarship fund that I set up in his name at a local community college. That's how people who knew William honored him—by doing what he would have done for me.

But William didn't let a thing like physical death get in his way of gift giving. He worked an amazing feat of his own, with a little help from a friend of mine, and had a very special delivery made to me that weekend.

When William's estate was being settled, his heirs sold off most everything that belonged to him—including many pieces of his beautiful home décor that we either picked out together or I gave him for birthdays and Christmases. I was not invited to the sale or offered any of his prized possessions as mementos, nor were his sisters or nieces that he loved so much.

Personally, I never had a hope to own anything that belonged to him. I was not even given the few personal items that belonged to me I had left there. But for some reason, all week before the sale, I kept conspiring in my head about who could help me get his bed. It was a king-size bed, and I didn't even know if it would fit in my bedroom. I never came up with a plan, so I let it go. But William must have heard me.

I believe he got a telepathic message to my friend, Linda. She called me, out-of-the-blue, which she does not often do, to say she thought she saw William's condo listed for sale in the newspaper. I confirmed that it was, and she said she thought she'd go look at it and check out the sale. I encouraged her to do so. She could tell me how it was going. Suddenly it occurred to me that this was the opportunity I had been rolling over in my mind! Linda became my little, secret-agent angel. As she walked through the condo that had once been William's beautifully-appointed home and my second-home oasis, she pretended to talk to her daughter on the phone, while telling me what was left of his furnishings.

Through Linda, my friend who loved William, I was able to purchase so many of the special items that we picked out together and some of the presents I had given him over the years. I had no problem paying for them a second time. Those precious belongings mean so much to me now and have made my home feel alive with his presence and his ever-flowing, loving energy. I was even able to get a couple of his things to share with his sisters. I am not sure if his bed was available, but it was probably best I did not get that item that we shared, even if it would have worked in my bedroom.

When I realized that his precious items were being delivered to me over Valentine's weekend, I understood fully that it was a sign to me that William had arranged a special delivery to happen at a special time for a special reason. I would always have these gifts in my home for all the Valentine's Days to come. I will never forget our love on that special day and this extraordinary Valentine surprise that meant the world to me.

~ Seven ~

Heavenly Scents

I Know That Smell

Sometimes smells associated with someone you lose have a physical source, and sometimes they don't. You may just smell the smell and not know where it is coming from—except in the air—or perhaps on a loved one you can't see in the same room with you. This is sometimes called an olfactory presence or clairalience or clairescence communication—having to do with the sense of smell and scents.

Powdery Fresh

On Thursday, June 4, 2008, I awoke from a nap on the sofa, sensing the presence of William. I didn't know if I had dreamed about him or what, but I could not remember a dream. Immediately, I smelled a distinct scent. It was the powdery fresh smell of a lotion that William had left in my bathroom. It was subtle at first, and I tried to figure out if the smell was from my own deodorant or something else. I tried smelling the pillows, but nothing around me held the scent, which came in three separate passes. One was more pronounced than the other two, as if it were on something or someone moving around.

The reason I recognized the smell was because five days before the experience, I had picked up the lotion bottle he left in my bathroom and smelled it for the first time since he'd been gone; had I not familiarized myself with the scent, I may not have recognized it as being associated with William. That was just more proof to me that I was right in my feelings that he had been around me all week. I think he saw me smelling it and thinking of him.

The following Tuesday after that new experience—June 9th—my friend, Dani, came over to meet me as we were going out for dinner. I still had my hair to dry, so she sat down on the sofa in the family room to wait for me. I was joking as I left the room, calling back, "If you smell a powdery smell, it's William." I didn't expect her to have the experience, but no sooner than I got the words out of my mouth, she said, "I smell a powdery smell!" She went on to say that it came and went and grew stronger at one point, which is exactly the way it occurred to me. I wrote in my journal that the powdery smell occurred at least three times during that week in June.

It was coming up on June 14—the date in 2007 of William's sudden seizure, which signaled the beginning of the end of our life together. Perhaps he just wanted to be close to me during what he knew would be a rough time for me to remember. He told me through the channeling experience that he would always come back around the time of my loss to help me through it. William was a man of his word. He made every effort while alive to keep his promises to me, and he made sure that didn't change. A promise is a promise, on earth and in heaven.

Burberry and Bologna

Even though William was not physically present, I often found myself walking around and talking out loud to him; however, I made sure I was not speaking loud enough so that other people could hear me and call for the men in white coats. On February 11, 2009, as I was on my way into the grocery store after yoga class, I thought about how much I missed William's wonderful, woodsy scent. He always exuded a sensual aroma.

So, on this particular evening as I thought about missing that element in my life, I said out loud to William, "I wish I could smell you, Babe. Let me smell you, okay?" I went on into the store where I was met with a virtual plethora of red, white, and pink—all sorts of Valentine's flowers, stuffed animals, and sweets everywhere. I had forgotten—twas' the season. I soon also forgot about my request of William… until I got around to the meat counter—the bologna aisle, to be specific.

I was staring at the polish sausage when, suddenly, I was overtaken by a very strong, familiar smell of William's favorite Burberry cologne! It was as if someone opened the bottle right under my nose! With no time to think, I spun around actually expecting to see him, I think. I scanned the area, looking for the source of the unbelievably strong smell I had just requested minutes before!!

There were only a few people in the vicinity, but I knew where the Burberry smell was coming from immediately. There was a well-dressed man who looked to be from India coming parallel to my location maybe twenty feet or more in front and to the right side of me—WAY too far away for me to have his cologne wash over me. I watched him as he walked on by, and a little voice inside my head said, "Go ask him what he's wearing, so people won't say you imagined it."

As soon as he stopped by the organic cereal display—still a good distance to the left and front of me now, I marched straight over to him and said, "Sir, excuse me, are you wearing Burberry Cologne?" He turned to me, looking very puzzled, and said, "Why, yes, I am." I was so excited as I told him my story. He looked sad and gave me his condolences, but I said, smiling broadly "No, I am so happy that he answered my request."

I smiled all the rest of the night. I said, "Wow, Babe, you can do anything!!" I was so thankful for my early 2009 Valentine 'presence'!! My prince is as amazing as ever!! He still loves surprising me with unexpected gifts.

Can you see how you get interaction with a loved one when you are open to it, and even more so, when you specifically *ask for it?* They can hear you. Talk to them. Ask for a sign, and pay attention for the answer to show up, because it will—maybe when you least expect it. And knowing they are still with you, will feel like the best gift ever.

~ Eight ~
Tuesday Morning
Two-Way Communication

I was beginning to notice a pattern in the communication between William and me. The medium connected us through a three-way conversation. After hearing from William in that environment and hearing him say he would always come back to be with me in the fall when my emotions would be affected by the traumatic memory, I knew that he was free to communicate with me at will.

After a time, I learned to talk to him more often and ask him for signs or help with specific things. That's when I realized that a more interactive communication style was possible between us. Like when I asked to smell him, and he responded by providing his cologne source so quickly.

Sometimes I would also ask him to help me around the house to figure out how to use tools to fix things. As soon as I would ask a question, I would hear a response in my head like, "Turn it around the other way." And I would immediately see clearly how it worked. Once I asked him, "How do you paint the inside of these bi-fold closet doors?" It was the only time in 26 years that they immediately popped off the track when I opened them. Now that they were flattened, I could see how to paint them. "OH! That's how. Thank you, Babe!"

Especially Strong Stationery

William had helped me with everything since the day I met him. I should have known that all I had to do was ask. So, one day I was going to our favorite shopping place, Tuesday Morning. As I was walking around, I began talking to him softly and telling him I didn't feel like he was there with me. I asked where he was. Immediately, I got the thought to walk over to the stationery aisle.

After a second I noticed a sign on the side of a box of fine stationery, William's name was hand-written in gold, and not just his first name, but his middle name as well—William Arthur. I was shocked! It was fancily written, very artistically, like his unique handwriting style. I felt he was letting me know he was there with me after all! I picked up the box to look at the notes more closely and was even more astounded!

William had been a very strong, 6'2 inch, 205-pound man of muscles when he was well. He was known for his great physical strength. That's why this particular box of stationery had his "name all over it," literally and figuratively. Not only was his name on the box, but at the very top of each piece of fine stationery in the box was the icon of a strongman in a red tank top holding up barbells—upon each was written "a ton."

The icon, itself, was very small. Underneath it in very small letters, like a whisper, it said, "Still a Ton of Fun." The first word out of my mouth was, **"STILL???"** Those words may have been small, but that message was LOUD and CLEAR. William was having as much fun now surprising me as he ever did on earth. I was so grateful for my message and so glad I reached out to him and that he answered me. We were actually having a two-way, interactive conversation now. I bought a box of the cards and headed home much happier than before I entered the store. William was there with me, after all.

The Family Silver

Another time in the same store—yes, it really was our favorite—which is probably why I gravitated back to it so often after William left me here to shop alone. Or did he? I had a similar experience as before in missing him at the store.

This time I asked him specifically for a sign that he was with me. Again, immediately I gravitated to an aisle where hidden beneath some cloth placemats was a box of silver placemats. If I had time to think about things, I might have thought I was on a hunt...to find a tie to William after the stationery find from the last trip yielded such a treasure.

I was about to find a new treasure. The silver placemats weren't the treasure—not in and of themselves. What was written on the box made them special and spelled out William to me. The manufacturer of the placemats was 'Sutton Place Silver!"

Last time, William showed me a product with his first and middle names on it, and this time I was led to a product that bore his last name! That was just amazing to me, and I can't see how I would have ever found Sutton Place Silver placemats buried under a pile without being led to their hiding place in the store. I was not looking for placemats, or for anything in that aisle, except the treasure that William wanted me to find!

A Neighborly Thing

A third time I went to Tuesday Morning with William in mind, the thought came to me that his neighbor, Brenda, would be in the store. She worked for the company but not in the store we visited. As soon as I walked in, I heard a voice from the back of the store, and though I don't think I had ever met her, I knew it was Brenda's voice.

Soon, a woman came to the front of the store, and when I asked if she was William's neighbor, she looked a little puzzled and confirmed that she was. We talked about William for a while, and she told me how much she missed him. I said that he must have known her sorrow and wanted me to say hello for him today because I thought of her before entering the store.

I think everyone who ever knew William misses him. His electric presence is hard *not* to miss. But for those of us who know we can still connect with him, he is as thoughtful, witty, and creative as ever.

~ Nine ~
Hello from Heaven
I Feel a Presence

I used to get a musical message from William almost every month. Maybe in Heaven Time, he was sending them on a daily basis, but time is much slower here on the earth plane, or so I have read. Music, however, was in the cards for this day.

On the morning of January 22, 2009, I had a dental appointment and was at the bathroom mirror in the process of getting ready when I suddenly had a strong feeling of William's presence. It was unusual because this time I was fully awake—rather than waking from a dream—and I don't usually know to expect him without a telepathic vision before-hand. While putting on my makeup, I would periodically pause and inquisitively ask, "William, are you here, Babe? Are you trying to tell me something?"

Right after asking him that question, I went over to my closet to get my clothes out to wear. Without a reason, I glanced up at the bookshelves to my right that William had built for me in the alcove outside my closet, and I noticed a book lying flat on the top shelf. I could not see what the title was, but I felt moved to reach up and pull it down, which I did.

The title surprised me—"Hello From Heaven!" by Bill and Judy Guggenheim. That was an eyebrow-raising moment. I was taken back a little since I was feeling that William was, indeed, trying to talk to me, and this seemed to confirm it. I opened the book randomly, as I often do with books to see what shows up as a message for me. This time I opened straight to a page within a chapter, titled 'Love is Forever.' It was all about helping your loved ones communicate with you!!

The first words I read in the chapter were, **"If you sense the presence of a deceased loved one while you are awake, consider the possibility that he or she may be trying to communicate with you verbally."** I was stunned, of course! I kept reading, and the authors suggested that we "ask for a sign to show you that your loved one still exists."

I had already experienced enough to know that William lived on, and I always look for signs of communication. I have proven to myself the benefit of asking questions of him and patiently waiting to observe an answer for when it is received. The book confirmed, as I have experienced, that some signs are more obvious than others, but the authors reminded me that the important thing is to **"trust your own intuition as to the meaning of the sign for you."** I wondered if that was my lesson for today, but it did not feel like William's intended message for me was complete.

As I was driving to the dentist, the feeling that William had something more to say to me persisted. I thought about what I had just read in the fortuitously-placed book with the ironically-relevant title and message, and I decided to ask William for a sign like the book had suggested.

"Speak to me in the music, Babe, like you've done before." At that very moment, I reached down and turned the volume up on the radio, which had been turned all the way down. It was tuned in to a non-local station—which baffled me, as I had never heard of it and have no idea why the radio wasn't on the station I always listen to.

A song was already playing. It was not familiar to me, but what grabbed my attention immediately was the other-worldly sound of the music—a haunting sound, like of angels singing. The words went something like this:

**"From the clouds in the skies, I will tell you" ….and
"Did you forget to tell me something?"**

I tried hard to catch and remember more words as I drove, but the only ones that stuck with me in this unusual song were about communicating "from the skies above." That definitely got my attention and prepared me for the song that came next, whose words were very meaningful and not likely to be forgotten, even in my highly-sensitive state of wonder and amazement at the morning's events. I just know that William was speaking directly to me!

Every word of the next song I was hearing for the first time was applicable to my situation, but here are some that hit my brain like a freight train—**"Stuck in reverse. And the tears come streaming down your face when you lose someone that you can't replace; could it be worse?"** The words were from Coldplay's song, "Fix You," and I think that is what William was trying to do—fix me, help me—maybe even fuss at me a little.

Though the words were new to me, every single one was being recorded and stored in the very cells of my body and soul this very first time. The initial song was my pre-message alert, so I would hear the second prophetic song in detail. I probably heard and remembered as much of the first song as was necessary to accomplish its purpose. William was simply saying "I am talking to you from heaven—listen up!"

William only initiated a message through a feeling of his presence so strongly this one time. I wasn't sure what specifically had caused this meeting, but I know he felt it was important to speak to me about my current situation. It was a kind of "Come to Jesus" meeting. I didn't pull over, but I probably should have. I was definitely not concentrating on driving my vehicle. The words accurately touched on every aspect of my life since William's physical absence left me groundless. The suggestion that I was not moving forward in any area of my life just about summed it all up. I guess he was spanking me with his new feathery wings.

My struggle in reinventing myself, career-wise; my inability to move past the memory of his all-encompassing love long enough to hold a vision of a new life for myself; choosing a "pretend" relationship with no chance of a future; drowning myself in tears much of the time I was alone; waking up in the early hours of the morning in fear of the future and sleeplessness. Evidently, he was seeing it all and feeling pretty sad about it.

He used the song to tell me that I was not going to be able to create a new life for myself if I **"stay too in love"** with him to let what we had go. The whole song is telling me that he is going to try and help me move on…to "fix" me. He says metaphorically that what is right for me will lead me to my purpose in this life and get me excited again.

William had been sending encouragement in many of the songs he alerted me to, but this time I felt it was different—more passionate, more frustrated. I think he was concerned about me and the choices I was both making and not making, to fill the void in my heart. He had made me feel so lovable in our time together, and he knew I was headed away from that feeling by engaging in an uncommitted and transitory relationship. He told me through the medium that "he had been in my life to show me what loved looked like, and now that I knew, I was not to settle for less."

I am pretty sure he could see that was exactly what I was doing. He was right; the inner child in me did eventually get hurt. And, unfortunately, it wouldn't be the last time. I am gullible in love. I don't understand when people don't tell the truth, and therefore, if I am in the game, my heart is there for the taking. And there will always be someone to take advantage of that, if I let them.

I always said that William loved me more than even my parents could have. I think that is because he knew me better than they did. I had been told he was my father in a past life, so I guess he had more time to figure out what I needed to be the best version of myself. William was always my biggest fan and supporter. He believed I could do anything, and seeing me stuck in the past, making no headway and few good decisions must have been hard for him. That is why I believe there was such a sense of frustration in getting through to me that day.

The song by Coldplay was a perfect song for his message, and after everything it took to get the message to me—not easy like at the gym where music is already playing—I definitely got what he was trying to say to me. Unfortunately, grief does not pack its bags so easily. And finding a prince like William did not get any easier either.

I am sure William could hear my heart-mind respond, "I hear you, Babe, I do. I just don't know how to let go of what we had. I am not ready to let the best relationship I could ever have imagined for my life leave my memory like it did my reality. I will do my best to thrive here without you. I will do my best to care about living—I promise. But I can't promise when you will see results."

That day, I could see how much energy it sometimes takes to get messages through to those of us stuck here in the slow, physical third dimension. William is pretty persistent as he always was, but I guess it could be pretty frustrating if we don't even believe or recognize that our loved ones are trying to talk to us. Believe for you. Believe for them.

~ Ten ~

William Dreams
Where Worlds Intersect

William Visits WVU

My then 18-year-old son, Cameron, was very close to William and left for college while he was sick. William never got to go to a single West Virginia football game or even visit to see where his buddy was going to school. One night after William died, Cameron said he slept on his dorm room floor. Maybe he was remembering all the times William napped on the floor at our house. When he woke up the next day, he said he could feel the presence of William's spirit there with him. He spoke to the presence he felt, saying, "How do you like my college, William?"

After the funeral, Cameron had a highly-vivid dream about William, again at WVU. He describes it this way:

"In my dream, I was walking down the streets of Morgantown and someone walked by, talking to his friends. He was saying that he had just lost someone named William Sutton, and if it wasn't for him, he would not have been able to go to college.

I went up to him and told him I knew William and that he dated my mom. He asked me if I was Cameron, and I said, 'Yes.' We started hugging and crying, and the person turned into William in his blue painter's shirt. We were both still crying, and he told me he loved me. He said, 'Thank you both (I assumed he meant Grayson, my brother) for coming to my funeral.' Then I asked him if he can hear me when I talk to him, and he said, 'Yes.'

The whole time I was dreaming, I felt like he was inside me or I was filled up with his spirit or something. Then, I woke up and called my mom and told her about this. I know he was really with me in my dream. I could feel it."

Because of the incredible vividness and orderliness of Cameron's dream, I believe it is possible that it wasn't a dream at all. He knew he was hugging someone that was no longer alive in the physical, and yet he could see and feel him in an experience that was not based on a memory. He asked real present-tense questions of him that he wanted answers to. The authors of "Hello From Heaven!," call this a "sleep-state after-death communication," and say they "feel like actual, face-to-face visits with loved ones." They also say they are "very similar to ADC's that take place while people are wide awake or in the twilight state."

I am not surprised at all that William would have gone to Cameron so soon; they were very close. Cameron accepted and loved William for who he was, and that meant the world to William. They worked together closely for several summers painting homes for William's painting business. It was Cameron's first job. The things William taught him about good work ethics, my son says he will carry with him always. Cameron later wrote an essay about William and his summer job for a college English course. It is a wonderful example of a true professional and how he taught and led by example for a young person. I am blessed it was my son. The essay is included in my first book, now titled, "Last Promise: Losing My Heart ~ Finding My Soul."

Denise and the Old, Oak Tree

William died 16 days before he got to turn 54 years old. I decided to throw him a "memorial birthday party" on the back deck at my home in honor of his beautiful life. Our friends, Suzy and Christian arranged for a big screen to be borrowed from their church, and one of William's dear friends, Vicki, made a DVD of photos of William to music that we played for all to see. I guess this was the deck party I asked William if he would come to after he painted my home. I am sure he was present that night. William loved a party, especially if he was to be the center of attention. Many of our friends and his family came, including my friend, Denise.

The next day, Denise surprised me by calling to say she had a strange dream about William, and she wanted to see if I knew what it meant. She felt that she was supposed to tell me about it. She said William had shown her a big tree with stepping stones around it. She wondered if I knew of a special tree around my house. I did! There was one—an ancient oak—that held a very special meaning for me. No other tree stood out in my mind. She suggested I go to the tree and see if I saw anything out of the ordinary. I didn't see anything.

In a couple of days the mystery was solved, and William's intention was clear. I received a greeting card in the mail from Denise with a big oak tree on the front. It's encouraging message was about being strong and standing tall through everything. It said that its limbs may be blown about, but its roots were firmly planted in the earth, and it was standing tall through it all.

I was astonished. Denise didn't know this, but William did. That was the last and exact same card that I bought for him near the end of his life, and it meant so much to him. I had been thinking about the card and lamenting over the fact that I left it in his home instead of taking it with me for safekeeping. Of course, I never got it back. I know the card that would have meant so much to me as a memory was thrown away as trash.

After Denise's dream about the big oak tree and William, she was led to buy the card and send it to me. Inside she wrote, "This card reminded me of the dream about you and William." She had no idea of my connection to and longing for that particular card, and she also could not have known the significance of her dreaming about a big oak tree and then finding and sending the card to me.

There is no question why William gave her the image of a big tree in a dream and why she thought she needed to tell me about it. He knew I'd understand how I got the card and why, when I did have it returned to me. I also believe he wanted me to know that the parallel between him and the strong tree standing tall through it all is still an accurate truth.

I will keep that card and the memory of it forever. It is an encouraging message I sent to him with love that he magically returned to encourage me by moving heaven and earth through a dream-like state, where worlds intersect.

~ Eleven ~

We Interrupt this Song
Merry Christmas

William doesn't occupy my mind for long bouts at a time like he used to do after he left and for many years after. It has been five years at this point. I am sure we are both adjusting to our worlds without each other. But sometimes, there he is again when I need him most. I believe he will always make himself known to me when I am thinking about him with a question or he hears me trying to figure something out that only he can answer for me. We don't lose our personalities, our souls, or our past memories when we leave here, and it is his nature and his path of many lifetimes to look after me. I know he still "has my back."

It was almost Christmas—December 21, 2012. I always think of him around special times. This day I was in the gym again. William doesn't show up there as much as he used to. But on this particular day, I was thinking about him and the end of our time together. I thought about how he was so aloof and detached emotionally from me at that time, and I wondered again if he stopped loving me after all we had meant to each other.

I thought about how his prayer partner and church mentor said that I was the Devil, and I couldn't help but wonder if she had been successful in turning him against me in the very end of his life when he was confused and upset. I felt that William believed in some way that he was being punished by God with his illness—like the biblical Job was in the last Bible story he read from start to finish. I hoped she hadn't made him believe that he was being punished for having me in his life.

I allowed myself to go back to times when I had disappointed William. I was feeling guilty about how upset he had been with me a few times over a business associate of mine that he did not trust. In light of how it affected him, I was sorry I had not honored his feelings more, even though I felt they were irrational at the time. I was apologizing to him while I was working out on the weight machines, telling him how sorry I was.

I had noticed they were playing songs from the 70's, and at times I sang along. Suddenly, the song stopped mid-track, and another song kicked in from another era. My antennae shot up immediately, as I sensed a meaningful event in progress, which was confirmed when the new song sounded an awful lot like a Ryan Cabrera song again!! It was almost like, "We interrupt our current song list for a very special message from heaven."

The song was an unquestionable response to my current thoughts of guilty memories, wondering if William still loved me. I never had a musical response to thoughts going through my head at the very same moment! I listened intently, as I knew the drill now. I would go home and search the internet on the words I could remember. I picked up the following most pertinent ones: **"Sick and tired of this world...I won't forget the way you loved me on the way down. You were all that I needed; all that I wanted."** I still have chills when I read those words remembering the sad mental state of despair I was in when I heard that song. It sure as heck sounded like William's reassurance in response to my current thoughts and concerns.

I knew then that he forgives me and wants me to forgive myself, or he wouldn't have popped in with such a relevant message so quickly. Even more powerful was the affirmation that I was always the only one for him, and he did not give up on us. Blaming ourselves for past actions is easy, and tying them to the reason a loved one gets sick or interpreting what they may have been feeling during such an emotional and irrational time is not a rational or healthy way to think or live. I believe that is why William was back again at the gym that day in December, working out in his special way, to speak to me in words from songs.

When I got home I found the song on the internet and, as expected, it was our new friend, Ryan Cabrera, singing his song, "On the Way Down." The entire song is an uncanny parallel to William in his last days and how he must have felt as he realized he would never have the chance to see his many dreams of a future come true, and we would never have the chance to have our happy ending. I know William knew how much I loved him and tried so hard to save him. He thanked me for everything I was trying to do for him one rare night when we were able to talk in the hospital before his energy got down so low.

I believe the Ryan Cabrera song delivers the message that William recognized and appreciated the love I showed him to the very end of his life here, and that is what he remembers and carries with him. I feel he is also saying that he would have given up much sooner if not for me and my belief that he would make it. The song says it all.

How amazing that the song even assures me that he is still alive!! He is letting me know he got through just fine and found words that actually express that while he was so afraid, he made it through to the Other Side okay, and he feels no burdens of the world anymore. **"It's alright, sunlight on my face; I wake up, and yeah, I'm alive."**

Once the song from 2004 ended, the track picked right back up where it left off—with songs from decades earlier—as if time had stalled and no one at the gym realized that anything had happened with the music. Well, no one but me and William. I continued my workout, smiling inside, knowing that William had gifted me with blessings of understanding, once again, from the Other Side.

~ Twelve ~

"You've Got Mail"

Old Messages, New Meanings

I always liked the Tom Hanks and Meg Ryan movie, "You've Got Mail." It was early in the game of technology when the movie highlighted a computer email program's voice that announced (and still does) whenever an email message popped up.

The day I "got mail" from William in heaven, I remember I was feeling very low. It happened on December 28, 2012, three days after Christmas and no doubt, I was having a pity party without the emotional stability of his great, big love in my life. I was alone and lonely. William spoiled me beyond measure, and the holidays were always the worse times to be without him. I was sorely missing his love in my life, and checking emails in my home office, which don't come with the voice announcement.

Certainly this email should have been announced as **"You've Got Mail—from Heaven!"** I clearly recall the foggy feeling of utter confusion when it appeared on the computer screen in front of me. How did I get back there in the archives of those old messages? I would have had to move the mouse to the top of the screen to reverse the viewing order of emails and even then, I would have had to select the specific email for it to open. I had done nothing to initiate a trip back six years into the past or land on a message from William. It just appeared, and it was dated September 21, 2006! It simply said:

"Good Morning Princess. Enjoy your day. The apple butter is great."

The shock of the message grabbed my attention because of its timing and relevance even more than wondering how all the steps to go back that far in my email system was managed without a keystroke. It was such a gift to hear him call me 'Princess' again, and it totally changed my mood and my energy for the day. I felt a smile cover my face. It made me feel loved at a time when I was missing it so much. It was also a sign that he knew my thoughts and was still there for me whenever I needed him to be, even five years after. I became joyful knowing that he was with me in such an amazing and mysterious way from the Other Side—a place I was more convinced than ever was just an arm's length or in this case…a keystroke away.

After I got that message from out-of-the-blue, I looked back through the archives to see what other messages still existed from William. The second email I read from him was dated September 11, 2006. I felt I was meant to get that message, as well. Not only was it relevant to my life at the time, but that email message was originated on the same date of William's death, only one year earlier.

The email subject head was, **"Can't Sleep."** The message from William read:

"Hey, I really enjoyed this weekend, even though a lot was involved with cleaning. We still have a sense of humor. I am glad you are being relieved of the headaches with the magazine. <u>I believe in your next success story</u>. Stay sharp for today's meeting. Love you Dee."

Those timely and supportive words were "so William." I couldn't help but smile through tears. He always believed in me and thought I could do anything. When I had him to believe in me, somehow I believed in me, too, and success was easy. I guess the messages that resurfaced that day were meant to encourage me, which they surely did.

I was feeling the effects of an uncertain future when I read William's second message to me that day. I had quit my job a month earlier and was to start yet another career in which I had no experience that very month. Nothing had felt right or been financially stable for me since I sold my magazine around the time when William became ill.

It was quite a day for email messages. I felt loved and supported in a way that only William could make me feel. Once again, he had successfully lifted me from the grieving doldrums, and loved me through to another day. Wow. I got so much more than mail that day!

~ Thirteen ~

As Time Moves On
My Big Move

I have no doubt that William will always be with me in ingenious ways when I call upon him or when I am thinking about him in sadness. However, I have read that as time goes on, our loved ones have other important things to do in their own evolution to higher levels toward Spirit in their new dimension. I know William was called up for something important, and I also know that I have to move forward, as well, to grow into my "new wineskins." Over time, I have called on him less, but he has shown me that he is always there for me whenever I really need him, no matter how much time has passed in our physical separation.

In March of 2014, I was faced with a necessary, but traumatic, downsizing of my home of 26 years. I guess it was time, but I went down fighting and screaming all the way. It was hard to leave because it was my family home and my dream home. I raised my children there and memories abound—both good and bad. I saw William happy there and sick and dying there. I was holding on to my past for dear life. It seemed like my memories were all I had.

I had made nature my new bundle of joy there on my acre and

a half—which I called my 'Hundred Acre Wood' since it sported that large, oak tree I mentioned in the earlier story. It had an opening in the bottom like Winnie the Pooh's door to his home, and I personally chose the lot to build our home on because of that tree. Leaving was a very emotional time; saying good-bye to the memories and all of my woodland animals that I had learned to love and enjoy so much.

Not knowing where I was going just made everything so much worse. I did not want to look out and see a parking lot from an apartment window after looking at spacious wood views, creeks, and a train that rambled through the woods. As a writer, I imagined I was like Henry David Thoreau when he escaped into the woods to write Walden Pond. I didn't want to wake up to the feel and sounds of the city. The thought of it brought tears to my eyes.

I called on God and all my angels and guides, the Archangels, Ascended Masters, Jesus, Buddha, all the people who loved me that had passed over, and anyone else unknown to me that could help. I needed an army of support from heaven—and I got it, not in Spades, but in Hearts. Mountains were moved, and at the last hour I landed in a cozy little microcosm of my beloved home—just seven minutes through the woods by foot! I found it miraculously online in the nick of time, simultaneously with my house going under contract after it had languished on the market for more than a year. Two other homes in my cul-de-sac had sold, literally, in days, and they were by the same builder with almost the exact same features as mine! But my house did not move.

As it turned out, if I had sold my house any earlier, the perfect, new place I found to call home would not have been available to me. In fact, it was only ready to be rented eight days before I had to be out of my house!! I was as close to being homeless as I could ever imagine and could see no way that I would end up happy anywhere else. As blind faith and the law of attraction would have it, I was the very first person to contact the rental agent/realtor who happened to actually own the condo I found online. Amazingly, he and his family lived in the same neighborhood as I did!! This was immensely helpful due to my unimpressive credit score I had accumulated over the previous few years and the lack of a job. What were the chances that the owner of my perfect, new home would be a current neighbor of mine??

Of all the places I had looked, it was the ONLY one I could see myself being happy in!! I went online often after finding it, mentally placing my furniture in each room shown. It all fit! It had every amenity that I had identified that would make me happy except a garage. I was so grateful that I never looked back with longing at the beloved home I left. I can't believe I still look out my windows and see trees and birds, a creek, and the very same train! The only difference is that I can now see and hear the creek from my open windows, and I don't have to stare hard into the woods to catch a glimpse of the train. I have it all, and even better than before!

I believe it is absolutely true that you must ask for help from the heavenly realm if you want or need them to intercede on your behalf, and after my experience, I won't be one to *ever* forget that or the knowing that faith the size of a mustard seed can move mountains for us. Please don't hesitate to ASK for help!

Bonnie, William, and the Table Leaf

As I was packing up to leave, I still had not found the leaf to my kitchen table. I had been looking for it forever! I remember a conversation with William about the best place to store it when he was alive, and I had not seen it since. I would only use it when my family came over for Christmas or Easter, and that's when it was really annoying not to know where it was. I had been "talking telepathically" to William about it for years with no help. As I said, his personality did not change, and William had good reason to ignore my request to find that leaf.

Antiquated, long-held ideologies about interracial couples by members of my family had kept William from having the seat he deserved at that table during those special holidays. In order to maintain holiday traditions for the children in our families, I regrettably allowed it. I am sure this was his way of making a statement about that wrong.

Well, near the end of the time in my house, I became a little more pointed about the table leaf in my "talks" to him. On a Monday near the end, I said, "Okay, William, this is it! You need to show me where that leaf is. I have looked everywhere that I can think of—in the attic, the garage, closets, behind furniture, under beds, everywhere. Where is it? I want to know TODAY!

Our good friend and my neighbor, Bonnie, changed the day she was coming to help me pack to that very day. We were in the small bedroom where she had decided to unload the single bookcase of all the books and photo albums. We were talking fondly about William and the nice things he had done for her and others. Bonnie thought William was a Saint even before he left the earthly realm. She said she could feel his positive energy when she stood next to him. He loved her, and she loved him. I could feel him smiling, just listening to all the praise.

Bonnie filled up all the boxes with books, and then she left. As I walked back into that room later on that day, I stopped dead in my tracks in front of the bookcase. I knew. "William, you didn't," I said!! But I knew he did. I went to the bookcase, which was not on the plan to be unloaded that day, and peeked behind it into the corner. There it was—the leaf to my table! On the very day I gave him an ultimatum, the leaf was recovered. I guess he knew it was time for that little game of hide and seek revenge to end. I would soon find it on my own. I am telling you—he has not changed a bit!!!

I can't believe how much I love my new, smaller place, considering the major resistance I put up in leaving my home. It's been more than a year, and I have never looked back. Even though William was not here with me in life, I have all of the pieces from his estate, which he was able to get to me for Valentine's Day, 2008. They fit in beautifully and make my home feel happily close to him in memory. I don't hear from him directly as much these days. I know it was time we both moved on, literally and figuratively, in our separate realms.

But, our love continues on in my heart...until next time. He will always be my prince, but I know he wants me to find a king to see me through to the end. So, I am open to receive that king into my life to love and love me for the rest of my life—one that in no way makes me settle for less than I deserve—and thanks to William—I know what that is.

Looking Back
William in Contemplative Mode—Greece, August, 2006

~ Fourteen ~

A Dose of Reality
Deathbed Promise

It took me four years to finish the first book I promised William, out-of-the-blue, on his deathbed the last night I saw him alive in this world. I truly feel he has been involved in helping me get it out there and promoting it because some absolutely, astonishing events have occurred with it. In fact, it was William who told me when it was time to release the book in a most amazing way. Here is my first-hand account as it actually occurred:

As I write these words, it is June 14, 2011. I saw the small piece of paper on the steps when I went up to bed last night, but I did not pick it up until this morning on the way back down. When I turned it over, I received a surprise—like so many others I have received from William—both before and after the physical separation we call death. The paper was a Christmas gift tag with the words, "To Dee: From William." Joy welled up in me; why would a Christmas gift tag from William show up on the stairwell of my home in June, four years after his passing? I did not know what the significance of the strange occurrence meant, but I knew it meant something.

With coffee in hand, I headed out to his favorite spot in my home—the screened-in porch—where I intended to meditate on it. I learned after William passed over that the porch is located in the 'Love' corner of the house, according to the rules of feng shui. Before I reached the door to the porch, I heard a voice in my head say, "Get a pen and notepad." I turned right around, having learned many times that failing to listen to my inner guidance system usually turns out to be the wrong way to go. You never know for sure who is speaking the thought in your head.

As I sit here, I take notice that the uncharacteristically cool day is filled with crisp fall air on this June morning, which felt like a typically hot day in the month of August just a couple of days ago. I try to keep my heart open by not crying, but tears stream down my face anyway. I hear William tell me that it is time. It is time to release the book, and it is time to release him and move forward with my life. Perhaps that is why I have been hiding the book I promised him in my computer instead of sending it out into the world. Maybe something in me believes I will be letting him go when I release the book. It has been edited so many times, and I could never feel sure it was perfect…..until today.

William has taken a stand, "It is time," he says, "Don't worry about where the book will go; it will find its own way to where it's supposed to be."

As I wrote those very words on the notepad, instantaneously, a thought occurred to me. William's shocking relapse was in June of 2007. So I stop my writing to search back through the manuscript for the actual date. What I uncover is the significance of finding the gift tag today. The final chapter of William's life began with a seizure ***exactly four years ago today—June 14, 2007.*** I knew then that William wanted to make certain there would be no question that he was sending me a message. A synchronicity with such relevance is hard to perceive as otherwise. Had I picked up the gift tag the night before, it would not have had the same impact.

Through Divine guidance, my gift on this autumn-like day in June is in knowing, without a doubt, that the book I promised William on that sad, autumn evening in September of 2007 is ready to meet the world. This gift of knowing was signed by his hand, "To Dee: From William."

My Gift Tag "Sign" From William

One month later, after being encouraged by a kind, internet stranger named **Joseph Dowdy** of California, whom I met through an online writer's group, I entered the manuscript in an international eBook contest and barely made the contest deadline by mere hours.

Later that month, I screamed in joyful shock when the announcement was made that William's story won a first place **Gold Global eBook Award in a Memoir category** and received **a Wow-Factor of 10** from judges!

Mr. Dowdy knew little about my story, but how very fortuitous that I would join a writer's group online for the first time ever and run into the managing director of a writing contest sponsored by Dan Poynter of ParaPublishing. And even more amazing that as a new author of my own book, I would win first place in a category of the contest!

I have been told that the book was channeled to me, and oftentimes, I feel that is the only explanation that makes sense. Current-day topics of conversation found their way into the book before they were "newsworthy." It is as though the book was ahead of its time, and the world had to catch up with it. I hear myself saying all the time, "Oh, my gosh—that's in my book!" I am always surprised, and often wonder how or why I stumbled upon some of the issues I did, and more importantly—what am I supposed to do with them?

What I found in writing the book was a belief that it was always in the Grand Divine Plan for me to write it. I did not consciously plan it on my own, though I was diligent in keeping a journal, writing down all the details surrounding William's health issue, researching voraciously, and taking pictures of his every move throughout the journey. I was a journalist without realizing it. What is truly inconceivable to me is that I stumbled into a research of cancer just weeks before William's diagnosis because of a topic I suggested for my son's high school science project that had nothing to do with the topic of cancer.

When my promise to write a book about him fell out of my mouth in a darkened hospital room as William lay in a coma, I felt someone else was speaking the words through me. I could only believe that the plan for that book and its subject was bigger than either William or me—but meant for us to fulfill together—and maybe even the reason we met on my doorstep, totally unaware, now almost twenty years ago.

By the time I finished the book, I could only feel that we had come together to help other people with my newfound knowledge about cancer, the issues surrounding it, and the business behind it that are affecting people's lives, largely without their knowledge. As William promised me on the screened porch that autumn-like day in June, the book has continued to find its place in the world on its own.

In 2012, an excerpt of the book was published by a German website publisher dedicated to natural healing modalities for cancer. And in 2013, I almost fell out of my office chair, literally, when I got an out-of-the-blue phone call from a London Magazine publisher who went out of his way to locate me after my old email "kept popping back." I had contacted the magazine a year earlier in response to a general request for health care stories that had gone badly, but never heard back from them.

The publishers featured William's story in their October, 2013 issue of the magazine, "What Doctor's Don't Tell You." Amazingly, William's photograph and his story were traveling to locations through Europe near the time of his earthly birthday that year, thanks to WDDTY publisher, Bryan Hubbard. I was so elated to be contacted by such a distinguished health and wellness publisher from the other side of the world. But beyond incredible to me was that after reviewing my book, Mr. Hubbard took it upon himself to get it into the hands of executives at a top international publishing house in London!

In the back of my mind, I hear the angel reader from four years earlier tell me that she felt the book had a better chance of getting published in Europe, and specifically, the UK! So, the backing of the angel realm can help those of us who are trying to help the world. My book has been reworked, updated with more resources, and the title has been changed to focus on the heart of the love story, which is to honor the life of an exceptional human being and help others before a scary diagnosis of cancer ever shows up around them. It is now titled, **"Last Promise: Losing My Heart ~ Finding My Soul."**

Even though I have not heard from the publisher in London, I have not given up hope for widespread distribution of the book as it makes its way to a wider audience. As William has already indicated— the book will get to where it is meant to be on its own, and it has already proven that. I am glad news of it has found its way to you here. There are no coincidences.

Where the Serendipitous Love Story Begins

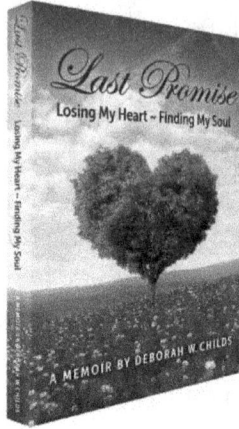

www.debwchilds.com
Available in print and eBook

~ Fifteen ~

What's Next for Me?

Divinely Inspired

In July, 2014 as I sat in my new home office contemplating my "next move," I received what felt like a message of Divine guidance. Nothing too unusual there—it's how I live my life. I noticed two books sticking out of my bookcase that I could not push back in. It could have been any old thing blocking it, since the office was still unorganized from the big move. When I pulled them out to see what was "behind the situation," I found Doreen Virtue's little book, called…. "Signs from Above"… and knew very well that this could actually be a sign *from above*! We are all privy to Divine guidance, but it requires awareness to recognize, or at least be curious enough to follow the thought when the possibility arises.

I opened the book at random to a story of a mother whose son had drowned and how a song from a CD he had bought her comes on the radio whenever she is thinking of him or asks him for a sign. Well, you know if you've read my story, thus far, that her experience with musical signs resonates deeply with me. I had been searching for a way to incorporate my spiritual beliefs into a path of inspiration and service to others. What might this "sign" have to do with that?

As I turned the book over, I discovered that Doreen Virtue and her son, Charles, facilitate worldwide Angel Therapy Practitioner certification workshops all over the world. Not bad for a woman who started out reading angel cards for people at a Whole Foods grocery store, or so I have heard. As would be the case with Divine guidance, Doreen was at that very time on the last leg of a workshop tour, which was said to be the first in a while, and possibly her last on location. Workshops were still scheduled for London, Maui, and Zurich for the next four months.

Sensing awareness of Divine guidance is not enough. It takes action to make things happen in your life. I first tried to make arrangements to be in London, but things were just not lining up. Besides, the economic exchange rate was very much to my disadvantage. Finally, things began to flow easily in a different direction. I found on Facebook a nice roommate and another new friend headed to Maui for the conference. So, I successfully made arrangements to be in spiritual Maui during William's earthly birthday in September of 2014!

I made plans to be spending time with other like-minded souls from all over the world who wish to help themselves and others navigate peacefully and productively through life in the earth realm by accepting heavenly help from angels and the Divine Spirit. Will a certification as an Angel Therapy Practitioner take me to where I want to be? I could not know; but there was only one way to find out! My plane arrived on the Island of Maui for my first visit to Hawaii on September 25, 2014.

Registered and Ready for Class!

I felt that I had William's blessings for my trip to Hawaii. My last few years of upheaval had taken me through a financial fire, and this felt like a just reward for selling my home and coming out on the other side. It was also an opportunity to expand my knowledge into a spiritual career. It did not take long for William to show me he was "with me" in spirit. As I sat on the plane to Atlanta, I struck up a conversation with two women in seats beside me. We chatted for a while before the subject went to why we were all headed to Hawaii.

They were both from Virginia, like me. Then the woman sitting right next to me mentioned she would be celebrating a birthday the next week. My antennae went up. Since William had a birthday the next week, too, I couldn't help but ask when her birthday was. I think I could feel it coming, but imagine my reaction to find that she was born on the EXACT same day *and year* as William!! What were the chances that she would be sitting next to me AND that the birthday information would come out in conversation? Normally, I don't even talk to people on planes.

On the next leg of the trip directly into Hawaii, I sat by a couple. For some unknown reason, the husband and I started chatting about things when his wife went to the restroom. Somehow we also got on talk of birthdays, and I told him about the strange birthday coincidence from the last plane. Again, I was shocked to hear that September 27th was also his wife's birthday!! I was speechless! There was absolutely NO DOUBT that William was with me all the way to Hawaii. He may not have arranged the airline seating, but he darned sure meant for me to know *who* I was sitting by and the significance of it.

At the angel intuitive seminars, we used angel cards to receive messages from the angels as we practiced our ability each day to intuit guidance from them for each other. During one of my readings, a dear woman started out immediately by saying she saw a big, red heart over my head; she then starting crying as she told me how much William loves me.

On a lighter and more humorous note, we had a meetup gathering during our conference in the form of a costume party where we were to dress up in any form of positive alter ego. I decided to go as a Transformer, the action star known as Optimus Prime. I was happy with my choice and on the way to the party, I asked my roommate, Linda, to snap a picture of me in my costume.

She tried several times, but the pictures were just awful—the lighting, the energy in my posturing, everything about it. Finally Linda called out loudly, "William, HELP US!" We laughed, and she tried again. Take a look at the "before the call for William's help" and the after results.

Before the call for help   …and after

I went from a limp-looking heroine to WONDER WOMAN in the blink of an eye at shutter speed! Linda, who was tired of trying and grateful to finally get a good shot of me, shouted, **"Thank you, William!!!"**

The difference between the photos was quite astonishing, and we found that both shocking and hilarious. I don't know if it was William's handiwork, the power of the spoken word, or a coincidence, but it was a very timely one, as usual. In any event, he would love to take credit for it—especially on his birthday! I guess he was ready for a party and came as photographic magician.

I am glad I was able to be in such a spiritual place on William's birthday with new friends of like-mind. And, though I missed him so much not being there with me physically, it was a blessing to have him with me in spirit, and I felt his presence often. Obviously, others did, too.

~ Sixteen ~

Ask and You Shall Receive

'A William' to Love

If you have trouble believing this story, I understand. I almost have trouble digesting it myself. But having experienced all I have since William passed over, I am a little less prone to shock over such phenomenal occurrences. Just when I thought I had penned the final chapter of this book, William seemed to have a few more messages to include on the idea about love and moving on.

I guess recalling all of the stories in this book about my prince was making me feel quite certain there was no way in the world I was ever going to find anyone nearly as perfect for me again. That is what I was feeling while standing in my kitchen close to 11am on August 28, 2014, and I said to him out loud, "William I want to move on; I do. But what are the chances of me finding a man anything like you? Do they even exist? They don't, do they?" I thought to myself—what are the chances of winning the jackpot of true, unconditional love twice in one lifetime?

I headed back to the table to finish editing this labor of love when I noticed a text message from a friend I had not talked to in more than a year. Stunned, I thought, "Laura?"

Take notice of the time and the text message, as you may not otherwise believe me.

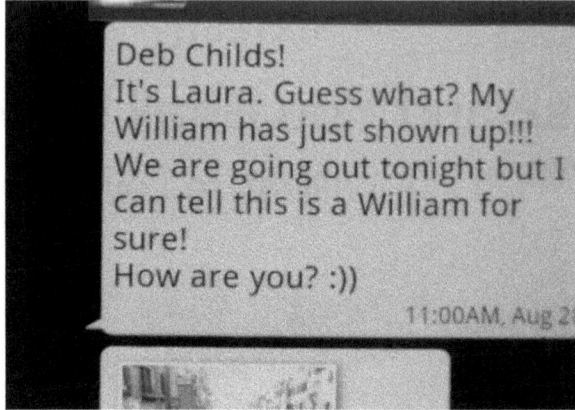

I could not believe my eyes. 'Did I *not just ask* if there were any more men like William in the world'!? Just to be clear, Laura's reference to 'a William' is a euphemism for a man who treats you like the princess you are; one who has the moral character and integrity to show you how lovable you are and to treat your relationship as a sacred, honorable agreement—like my William did for me.

Of course, compatibility has a big role in it after the values quotient is in alignment. Laura was only at the beginning of her relationship journey with this man. Whether or not her date would be 'a William' for her was not the extraordinary issue here. What was so amazing is that *at the very moment* I am expressing my doubts on the idea of the existence of men like William, I instantly receive a message to the contrary from someone I haven't heard from in a year who believes she has found one!!

Laura and I had never talked about finding 'a William,' so I was surprised to read that term in her text. I called my friend immediately to catch up and tell her about the synchronistic timing of her odd text message. She explained that about two weeks ago she was looking through a book I loaned her and saw that I had made a list of my intentions in the back of the book. My number five intention was:

"I have found my new William, perfect for me in every way."

Laura said, "I was going to call you when I read it, but I got busy and put it off. But today, the feeling to pick up the phone was so strong, so I sent you a text to let you know what's going on. If I hadn't read what you wrote in the book about finding your "new William," I don't think I would have thought about the request for a date from this handsome man I just met in the same way. Your energy was in the book."

I guess our story of a fairy-tale beginning helped Laura believe in the possibility of magic, and she was able to say yes to a man she just met who was culturally different from her. I assume William wants me to be open to possibilities the way Laura had, as she seems to be the bearer of that message for me today with a text message that was a direct response to my rhetorical question only moments earlier!

I suppose there is hope for me yet, as long as I don't give up. I think that was what William wanted me to hear from Laura—that it *is* possible, and we can only know by stepping out into the ring again. I am open to receive new love. I am open to receive new love. I am open to receive...

Another Girlfriend with a Message from William

When I heard the voicemail message from my friend, Jan, I could hear a hint of excitement in her voice. I called her back and said, "You have something to tell me, don't you?" She giggled and said she did. "William came to me in a dream, and he gave me something to give you," she said. I was all ears. Jan told me that William had a big box with two smaller boxes inside. The first small box had wedding rings in it for me, and the second one had a groom's ring in it. She said he had a man with him that she thought was meant for me. She interpreted William to be saying it was time for me to get married. I started to cry.

Jan felt the dream was so vivid that she knew she would not be able to forget it, but she couldn't wait to tell me about it. It certainly seemed like William was encouraging me to move on to love in my life, and here he was talking to my girlfriends again. I told Jan that he came to her because she is in sales and is constantly networking her way to success and meeting large numbers of people. She is the one out in the world, and that's probably why William came to her. I told her she needs to keep me in mind when she is working the streets of business. We laughed, and she thought maybe I was right. But there can be no mistake that William wants me to live my life fully, and that includes a loving relationship.

One More Valentine's Day Message

With all these love messages from William over the past few months telling me to move on, my Valentine's Day, 2015 seemed pretty glum and a bit sad. It was an emotional one as I was missing William more than ever. Did I realize it would soon be good-bye for real? Was new love in my cards?

In the wee hours of Valentine's Day morning, I decided to use my angel cards created by Doreen Virtue to submit a request to the Archangels ever present in our lives to help us. After all, I am a certified Angel Therapy Practitioner now! I learned from my course in Hawaii that angels have no authority over our free will and are constantly awaiting our call for their help. They are God's messengers, but they cannot intervene—except in emergencies—unless we ask them. So, on this sad morning of yet another Valentine's Day without my Valentine, I asked the angels to please give me a message from William.

I personally draw five cards when I call on the angels for assistance, but on this particular draw there was really only one card that I was looking for. One card in the deck of 45 cards speaks of a message from those in heaven, and it is aptly called—Hello from Heaven. All the cards showing up were good ones, but I had gotten through four of the five in my draw, and I was feeling like I would not get the message I wanted from William. When I turned over the last card—THERE IT WAS!!!!

Hello from Heaven

"Hello from Heaven! Your loved ones in Heaven are doing fine. Let go of worries, and feel their loving blessings."

That was exactly what I needed to hear. I went to bed and slept soundly all night.

Afterword

It's Your Turn Now

In closing, if you still do not believe in Divine guidance, life-after-death, angels, or the potential to communicate with deceased loved ones, then sadly, those possibilities will probably not be part of your life experience because you will not seek them to be. I am not a fiction writer, nor could I have ever imagined all of these perfectly-timed and relevant events, thoughts, and messages from music, fortune cookies, old emails, books, smells, stationery, silver placemats, phone calls from strangers, dreams through others, text messages, and angel cards. But imagination was not a necessary ingredient for these messages to be received—it only took the ability to be open and the willingness and desire to notice them. That's all.

Everything in the universe is made up of molecules of energy— and that includes you, me, and our loved ones who have passed over. Right now, they are on a different wave length of energy or channel of frequency than we are. But communication is possible if we can tune in to the same station. **Pay attention. Practice listening. Be patient. Seek help. Notice what you notice. Open your heart. Let down your defenses. Look for the signs. Enjoy all there is of the energy of life.**

As the previous chapter title suggests—Ask and You Shall Receive. Those words are straight from the lips of Jesus, according to the Bible, and that should be your quest. Ask for the guidance that you want, and be open to receive it! It is truly a choice—simply a decision to be made.

If grief or sadness from loss is a part of your life, I hope my experiences will give you some solace and knowledge that new joy lies in the midst of your sorrow. But only you have the ability to accept it. I hope my stories help you do that by creating your own stories with loved ones present—and opening up to those who have passed over. Separation is difficult, but it certainly helps to know that love and life are forever. We will be together with our loved ones again, in spirit and maybe even in the physical—if you believe in twin souls and soul mates reincarnating. But while we still have the blessing of life, we must live it to the fullest potential from the seen and unseen worlds around us. God bless you on your path; may it take you to beautiful places.

Thank you for reading my book! If you enjoyed it, I would greatly appreciate it if you would take the time to write a short review about your reading experience at amazon.com so others may be inspired to read it also. But first, continue on for information on your special gift and more about my first book where our love story with a purpose begins in Last Promise: Losing My Heart ~ Finding My Soul.

I truly hope you will want to keep in touch with me at www.debwchilds.com for future offerings, angel readings, and to share future stories. For example, here's something that came up from the spirit world after I put the final ink on this book.

NEW, UNPUBLISHED STORY

Right after my "Laura experience" in Chapter Sixteen, I received another shocking surprise with a communication tip from the spirit world. I decided to go ahead and finish the book and save this story I call **"The Enlightening Lunch,"** with a "special tip" for readers who want to be in contact with loved ones in heaven and are interested in continuing contact with me, too!

Keep reading for the opportunity to receive the astonishing story that illustrates how Divine guidance revealed to me a secret about a tool that was already helping me—without my awareness—to connect to William all these years! Information is included on how you can get one for yourself. Authentic versions come from only ONE PLACE IN THE WORLD and can help you make connections between heaven and earth.

I believe with all my heart that William and I met for a reason in this lifetime. I am also positive that our amazing love was supposed to lighten the burdens of others and empower them with our story and all we learned through our experience of love and loss. I consider it my highest calling, and I would be extremely honored if our story could help you or your loved ones. **For more information, please visit www.debwchilds.com.**

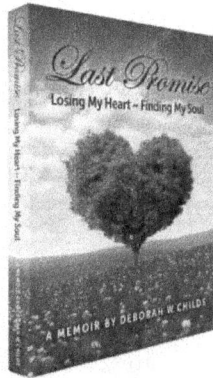

"Like a clip of amnesia, a flood of familiar feelings washed over me with no memories to back them up as I stood there dazed. As regular time kicked back in, and the painter looked up at his prospective customer, neither could have known the twist of fate that would alter their lives forever."   **---Book Excerpt**

Praise and Raves from Around the World for...
Last Promise: Losing My Heart ~ Finding My Soul

A Gold Award Winner with a Wow Factor of 10 from Judges

"Childs has a fluid writing style that is easy to read. I was able to read it in a two-hour sitting. The love story is touching and believable...a fascinating telling... a good read indeed."
---Judge, Global eBook Awards

"It has been said that if you want to change your life, fall in love. Deborah Childs fell in love and her life became the narrative for this touching book. Her capacity to love has made her both a great storyteller and an outspoken health care advocate."

Tim Reid, actor, director, producer, cancer survivor, author of *Dream Chaser—The Life and Times of Tim Reid*

"This is an extraordinary journey of love and loss, and the deep and profound lessons both can teach us. Deborah Childs writes beautifully and is a compassionate guide as she takes you through her story, her battles with an uncaring medical establishment, and finally her own resolution."

Bryan Hubbard, Publisher, *What Doctors Don't Tell You,* *wddty.com—voted most popular health website in the UK;* **Author of** *The Untrue Story of You — London*

"This book is one of those special books that everyone, in some way, can relate to and be touched by. Deb Childs has obviously put her heart and soul into her work, and the result is a true inspiration to any reader. Very few books lead you to feel the heart of the writer as this one does. Do yourself a favor and read this wonderful work of Deb Childs."

M.A. Cole—author of *Love, Ms. Grace*

"No one can imagine what it is like to face the daunting and unknown journey of what it feels like to be told you have cancer and not know all the obstacles you will face. Each person's journey is unique, but Deb Childs shares her story in a way that anyone facing a similar battle can glean knowledge and compassion from......she puts a face on a subject most want to ignore. She makes us remember that cancer is about the many people it takes from us...."

**"Anyone with a loved one facing cancer needs
to read this book!"
Vicki Ferris— Amazon 5-Star Review**

Other Reader Testimonials—

"This is a beautiful love story with valuable lessons for us all."

"I went to bed and had to get back up and finish reading it."

"I cried through your book…such an amazing love story."

"I couldn't put it down"

About the Author

After six years as the publisher of KLEOS, a Richmond business magazine reporting on excellence in the region, Deb Childs' world was turned upside down by the devastating diagnosis and eventual loss of her soul mate to cancer. Her journey after that tragedy led to a deepening of her spiritual awareness and the desire to use her writing talent to inspire others by documenting life stories. She is an award-winning author and ghostwriter whose own personal experience with loss drove her to become an avid health care advocate.

Because of the grief and fragmented life she experienced in the aftermath of her loss, Deb is passionate about leading others to personal empowerment through education and healing by teaching others to intuitively receive their own inner guidance with added assistance from the angel realm. Through an intensive study with world-renowned, best-selling author, and spiritual doctor of psychology, Doreen Virtue, Ph.D., Deb became a certified Angel Therapy Practitioner (ATP) in 2014. She instructs others to be an open channel for Divine communication, as well as, the grief-healing messages and support from transitioned loved ones to gain the clarity and wisdom needed to move forward to fruitful lives.

Childs' first release was an international award-winning book, *A Dose of Reality,* now updated and retitled, *Last Promise.* In her follow-up work, Childs adds her uplifting experiences of reconnecting with her loved one over the years following his transition in a new book, *A Spirit in the Doorway.* She hopes to enlighten others to the knowledge and real possibility that communication with departed loved ones can be a source of great comfort.

Childs has two beloved sons and lives in Richmond, Virginia where she enjoys nature photography and inspiring others to life beyond the illusion of five senses. Visit www.debwchilds.com

Other offerings from the author:

Deb blogs and inspires as a speaker on the following topics of Personal Empowerment:

- Angel Therapy—Getting Help from the Angelic Realm
- Divine Guidance: How to Recognize and Follow It
- Getting Unstuck from Grief by Connecting with Loved Ones On the Other Side
- 'Feeling it Real' Manifesting Success Stories and How to Create the Life You Want
- Intro to EFT—Emotional Freedom Technique—A Way to Lose Anxiety Fast
- Take Back Your Well-Power!
- Healthy Ways to Engage and Strengthen the Doctor Within
- 10 Optimal Ways to Avoid and Lose the Fear of Cancer
- Hippocrates 101: After a Cancer Diagnosis—What's Next?
- How to Advocate for Those You Love with Cancer

Contact Deb to: Deliver powerful keynotes for empowering women's seminars, an inspiring kick-off for special events, half-day teaching programs, and short healing angel card readings at lunch to inspire

For more information, visit: www.debwchilds.com

Other ways to connect with Deb:

Website and Blog: www.debwchilds.com

Email: deb@debwchilds.com

LinkedIn: www.linkedin.com/DebChilds

Facebook: www.facebook.com/ADoseofReality.William

Twitter: twitter.com/@lifeintention

HERE IT IS—

Your free copy of "The Enlightening Lunch" and information on a tool to help you connect with your loved ones on the Other Side

www.debwchilds.com/gift

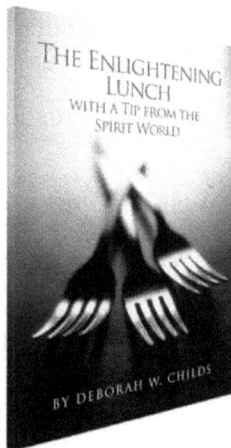

Remembering Dr. Wayne Dyer

The teacher whose spiritual wisdom put me on my path to enlightenment, opened my mind, and altered my view of reality for the better.

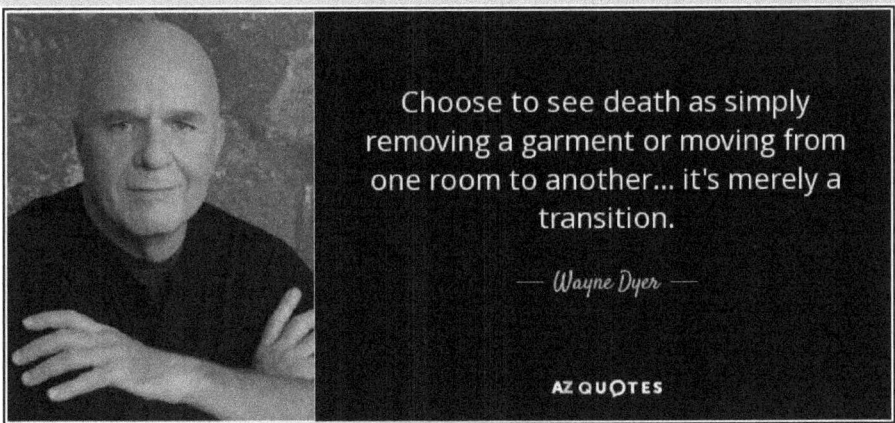

Choose to see death as simply removing a garment or moving from one room to another... it's merely a transition.

— Wayne Dyer —

AZ QUOTES

May 10, 1940 – August 29, 2015

Your work—and you—live on; but still, we will forever miss your presence on earth.